Practice Test #1

Physical Sciences Practice Questions

1. Which of the following tend to increase the melting point of a solid?
   I. Increasing molecular weight
   II. Decreasing polarity
   III. Increasing surface area
   a. I and II
   b. II
   c. III
   d. I and III

2. One mole of oxygen gas and two moles of hydrogen are combined in a sealed container at STP. Which of the following statements is true?
   a. The mass of hydrogen gas is greater than the mass of oxygen.
   b. The volume of hydrogen is greater than the volume of oxygen.
   c. The hydrogen and oxygen will react to produce 2 mol of water.
   d. The partial pressure of hydrogen is greater than the partial pressure of oxygen.

3. One mole of an ideal gas is compressed to 10 L and heated to 25 °C. What is the pressure of the gas?
   a. 2.4 KPa
   b. 2.4 atm
   c. 0.2 atm
   d. 0.2 KPa

4. Which of the following statements is true about the physical properties of liquids and gases?
   I. Liquids and gases are both compressible
   II. Liquids flow, but gases do not
   III. Liquids flow, and gases are incompressible
   IV. Liquids flow and gases are compressible
   V. Gases flow and liquids are incompressible
   a. I and III
   b. II and IV
   c. III and V
   d. IV and V

5. 1 mole of water and 1 mole of argon are in a cylinder at 110 °C and 1 atm of pressure. The temperature of the cylinder is reduced to -5 °C. Which statement about the contents of the cylinder is most accurate?

    a. The pressure in the cylinder is decreased, and the partial pressure of argon is less than that of water.

    b. The pressure in the cylinder is about the same, and the partial pressure of water is less than that of argon.

    c. The pressure in the cylinder is decreased, and the partial pressure of water is much less than that of argon.

    d. The pressure in the cylinder is decreased and the partial pressure of water is the same as argon.

6. Silver nitrate ($AgNO_3$) is dissolved in water. One drop of an aqueous solution containing NaCl is added and almost instantly, a white milky precipitate forms. What is the precipitate?

    a. NaCl

    b. $NaNO_3$

    c. $AgNO_3$

    d. AgCl

7. Comparing pure water and a 1 M aqueous solution of NaCl, both at 1 atm of pressure, which of the following statements is most accurate?

    a. The pure water will boil at a higher temperature, and be less conductive

    b. The pure water will boil at a lower temperature and be less conductive

    c. The pure water will boil at a lower temperature and be more conductive

    d. The pure water boil at the same temperature and be more conductive

8. 50 grams of acetic acid $C_2H_4O_2$ are dissolved in 200 g of water. Calculate the weight % and mole fraction of the acetic acid in the solution.

    a. 20%, 0.069

    b. 0.069%, 0.20

    c. 25%, 0.075

    d. 20%, 0.075

9. One liter of a 0.02 M solution of methanol in water is prepared. What is the mass of methanol in the solution, and what is the approximate molality of methanol?

    a. 0.64 g, 0.02 m

    b. 0.32 g, 0.01 m

    c. 0.64 g, 0.03 m

    d. 0.32 g, 0.02 m

10. A material has a half life of 2 years. If you started with 1 kg of the material, how much would be left after 8 years?

    a. 1 kg

    b. 0.5 kg

    c. 0.06 kg

    d. 0.12 kg

11. Which of the following statements about radioactive decay is true?
   a. The sum of the mass of the daughter particles is less than that of the parent nucleus
   b. The sum of the mass of the daughter particles is greater than that of the parent nucleus
   c. The sum of the mass of the daughter particles is equal to that of the parent nucleus
   d. The sum of the mass of the daughter particles cannot be accurately measured

12. Hund's rule regarding electronic configuration states:
   a. Electrons in the same orbital must have an opposite spin
   b. Electrons must fill lower energy orbitals before filling higher energy orbitals
   c. Electrons must populate empty orbitals of equal energy before filling occupied orbitals
   d. Electrons must have the same nuclear spin as the nucleus

13. Arrange the following compounds from most polar to least polar:
$$F_2, CH_3CH_2Cl, NaCl, CH_3OH$$
   a. $NaCl > CH_3OH > CH_3CH_2Cl > F_2$
   b. $F_2 > NaCl > CH_3OH > CH_3CH_2Cl$
   c. $CH_3OH > NaCl > F_2 > CH_3CH_2Cl$
   d. $NaCl > F_2 > CH_3OH > CH_3CH_2Cl$

14. What is the chemical composition of ammonium sulfate?
   a. N 21%, H 3%, S 24%, O 32%
   b. N 10%, H 6%, S 24%, O 60%
   c. N 10%, H 4%, S 12%, O 74%
   d. N 21%, H 6%, S 24%, O 48%

15. Calculate the mass of water produced from the reaction of 1 kg of n-heptane with oxygen.
n-heptane (1 kg) + 11 O$_2$ → 7 CO$_2$ + 8 H$_2$O
   a. 144 g
   b. 8 kg
   c. 800 g
   d. 1.4 kg

16. The overall reaction A→D can be described by the following equation:
$$A \xrightarrow{\text{fast}} B \xrightarrow{\text{slow}} C \xrightarrow{\text{fast}} D$$
What would be the rate law for the overall reaction of A to D?
   a. Rate = k[D]/[A]
   b. Rate = k[B]
   c. Rate = [B]
   d. Rate = k[C]/[B]

17. Which of the following are considered Lewis acids?
      I. H_2SO_4
      II. $AlCl_3$
      III. PCl_3
      IV. $FeCl_3$
   a. II and IV
   b. II and III
   c. I and IV
   d. I and II

18. What is the pH of a buffer containing 0.2 M NaOAc and 0.1 M HOAc? The pka of acetic acid is 4.75.
   a. 4
   b. 5
   c. 6
   d. 7

19. 100 g of NH_3 are cooled from 100 °C to 25 °C. What is the heat change for this transition? The heat capacity of ammonia gas is 35.1 J/(mol) (°K)
   a. -263KJ
   b. 15.5 KJ
   c. -15.5KJ
   d. 263 KJ

20. Which of the following molecules are alkenes?

   a. I
   b. II
   c. III
   d. IV

21. Methyl mercury is a toxin produced indirectly from what energy source?
   a. Oil
   b. Natural gas
   c. Wood
   d. Coal

22. The masses of four different objects taken with different scales were 23.04 g, 7.12 g, 0.0088 g and 5.423 g. What is the total mass of all four objects to the proper number of significant digits?
   a. 35.59180
   b. 35.5918
   c. 35.60
   d. 35.59

23. Consider the two vectors below:
Vector A:

Vector B:

Which vector best represents the vector obtained by subtracting A from B ($\vec{B} - \vec{A}$)?

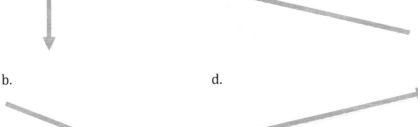

a.

c.

b.

d.

24. You throw a baseball straight up near the surface of Earth and it falls back to the ground. Which statement is true about the acceleration of the baseball at the top of its path? [Ignore air resistance]
   a. The acceleration is zero.
   b. The acceleration changes sign.
   c. The acceleration is -9.8 m/s².
   d. The acceleration continues to increase.

25. Consider the following statements about Newton's law:
I. A newton is a fundamental unit.
II. Mass and acceleration are inversely related when the force is constant.
III. Newton's first law can be derived from Newton's second law.
IV. Newton's second law can be derived from the universal law of gravity.
Which of the following statements are true?
   a. I, II, and III.
   b. II and III only.
   c. III only.
   d. I, II, III, and IV are not true.

26. In an amusement park ride, you stand on the floor of a cylindrical ring with your back touching the wall. The ring begins to rotate, slowly at first, but then faster and faster. When the ring is rotating fast enough, the floor is removed. You do not slide down but remained pressed against the wall of the ring. Which is the best explanation for why you don't fall down?
    a. The centripetal force pushes you towards the wall.
    b. The centripetal force changes the direction of your motion.
    c. The force of friction between the wall and your body is greater than your weight.
    d. The rotating ring creates a weightless environment.

27. A 10-kg plastic block is at rest on a flat wooden surface. The coefficient of static friction between wood and plastic is 0.6 and the coefficient of kinetic friction is 0.5. How much horizontal force is needed to start the plastic box moving?
    a. 5 N
    b. 49 N
    c. 59 N
    d. 98 N

28. The pulley in the device below has no mass and is frictionless. The larger mass is 30 kg and the smaller mass is 20 kg. What is the acceleration of the masses?

    a. 0.5 m/s²
    b. 2 m/s²
    c. 9.8 m/s²
    d. 98 m/s²

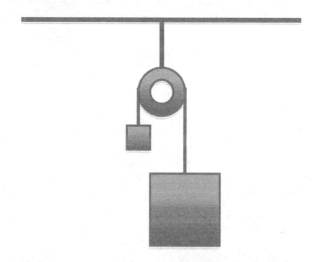

29. Two unequal masses are balanced on a fulcrum using a massless bar, as shown below. If both masses are shifted towards the fulcrum so that their distances from the fulcrum are one-half the original distance, what happens to the masses?

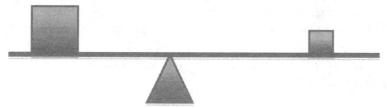

    a. The heavier mass will tilt downward.
    b. The masses will remain balanced.
    c. Cannot be determined from the information given.
    d. The lighter mass will tilt downward.

- 8 -

30. Impulse is measured as the change in an object's momentum. Which statement is correct about the impulse on a ball rolling down a hill? Ignore air resistance and friction.
    a. The impulse is constant.
    b. The impulse only exists for a short time.
    c. The units of impulse are joules per second.
    d. The object's impulse increases.

31. A 75-kg ice skater moving eastward at 5 m/s collides with a 100-kg skater moving northward at 4 m/s. Anticipating the collision, they hug each other and produce an inelastic collision. What is their final speed?
    a. Can't be determined from the information given.
    b. 3.1 m/s
    c. 4.1 m/s
    d. 2.1 m/s

32. Which statement correctly states the work-energy theorem?
    a. The change in kinetic energy of an object is equal to the work done by the object.
    b. The change in kinetic energy of an object is equal to the work done on an object.
    c. The change in potential energy of an object is equal to the work done by the object.
    d. The change in potential energy of an object is equal to the work done on an object.

33. A ball is released from a certain height along a frictionless track that does a loop-the-loop. The loop-the-loop part of the track is a perfect circle of radius R. At what height above the ground must the ball be released from in order to not fall off the track when it gets to the top of the loop-the-loop?
    a. R
    b. $2R$
    c. $\frac{5R}{2}$
    d. $3R$

34. Which of the following statements about energy is true?
    a. Mechanical energy is always conserved in an isolated system.
    b. Total energy is always conserved in an isolated system.
    c. Energy is never created or destroyed.
    d. You can determine the mechanical energy of an object by using $E = mc^2$

35. Which of the following statements best explains what is meant by the phase of a wave?
    a. The height of a wave in 2π radians.
    b. The length of a wave in 2π radians.
    c. The period of oscillation of a wave.
    d. An angle indicating the wave cycle's instantaneous location.

36. Which of the following statements is true about the acceleration of a simple pendulum?
    a. The acceleration is constant.
    b. The magnitude of the acceleration is at a maximum when the bob is at the bottom of the path.
    c. The magnitude of the acceleration is at a maximum when the bob is changing directions.
    d. None of the above.

37. Two waves, each of which has an amplitude of A, cross paths. At the point where they cross, the peak of one wave meets the trough of another wave. What is the resulting amplitude at the point where the waves cross?

    a. 0
    b. A
    c. 2A
    d. -A

38. Two tuning forks have a frequency of 500 Hz and 504 Hz and the same amplitude. How much time is there between beats?

    a. 4 seconds
    b. 15 seconds
    c. 0.25 seconds
    d. 2 seconds

39. Substance A has a density of 5.0 kg/m³ and substance B has a density of 4.0 kg/m³. What is the ratio of the volume A to volume B when the masses of the two substances are equal?

    a. 1.25
    b. 0.80
    c. 1.12
    d. 0.89

40. The center of a circular aquarium window with a radius 1 meter is 14 meters below the surface. What is the force of the water at this depth pushing on this window? The density of water is 1000 kg/m³.

    a. 1.37×10^5 newtons
    b. 1.08×10^5 newtons
    c. 4.3×10^5 newtons
    d. 0 newtons

41. The air passing over an airplane's wind is considered an irrotational fluid flow. Which of the following statements correctly describes the concept of irrotational fluid flow?

    a. The fluid flows in a straight line.
    b. All particles have the same velocity as they pass a particular point.
    c. A tiny paddle wheel placed in the fluid will rotate.
    d. The fluid does not have any rotating points, whirlpools or eddies.

42. Which statement best explains why water expands when it freezes?

    a. The coefficient of thermal expansion is negative.
    b. The average distance between the water molecules increases.
    c. The density of water is greater at higher temperatures.
    d. The internal energy of the water decreases.

43. Which of the following statements best describes the electric field shown below.

    a. The field is decreasing down.
    b. The field is decreasing to the right.
    c. The field is increasing to the right.
    d. The field is uniform.

44. An electric field is pointing from south to north. If a dipole is placed in the field, how will the dipole's orientation change?
    a. The positive charge will be on the northern side and the negative charge will be on the southern side.
    b. The positive charge will be on the southern side and the negative charge will be on the northern side.
    c. The positive charge will be on the eastern side and the negative charge will be on the western side.
    d. There will be no change in the orientation.

45. A magnetic field is directed into this page and an electron is moving from left to right as indicated in the diagram below.

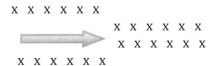

In which direction will the electron move when it enters the magnetic field?
    a. It will curve upward.
    b. It will curve downward.
    c. It will curve in the direction of the magnetic field.
    d. It will curve in the direction opposite the magnetic field.

46. In the 19th century, James Clerk Maxwell calculated the speed of light in a vacuum from the proportionality constants used in electrostatics and magnetism. Which of the following relationships correctly identifies how light moves in a vacuum?
    a. High frequencies of light travel faster than low frequencies.
    b. Low frequencies of light travel faster than high frequencies.
    c. All frequencies of light travel at the same speed in a vacuum.
    d. Light moves at infinite speed through a vacuum.

47. The diagram below shows two batteries connected in series to a resistor. What is the direction of current flow?

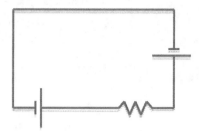

a. clockwise
b. counterclockwise
c. neither clockwise nor counterclockwise
d. Can't be determined from the information given.

48. A circuit consists of a battery and a resistor. An ammeter is used to measure the current in the circuit and is connected in series to the circuit. Which of the following is true?
a. The current flowing in the resistor increases.
b. The current flowing in the resistor decreases.
c. The voltage drop across the resistor increases.
d. The current flowing in the resistor remains the same.

49. A capacitor is connected in series to a battery and a resistor. The battery is disconnected after the capacitor is charged and replaced by a battery with a greater electromotive force, causing the capacitor to gain additional charge. After the capacitor has fully charged again, which of the following statements is true about the capacitance of the circuit?
a. It has increased.
b. It has decreased.
c. It has remained the same.
d. It has become zero.

50. A homemade generator rotates at a constant frequency and produces an alternating current with a maximum voltage of 40 volts. It is connected to a resistor of 20 ohms. What is the average current that flows through the resistor?
a. 0 amperes.
b. 1.4 amperes
c. 2.0 amperes
d. 2.8 amperes

51. A ray of light travelling in a vacuum (n = 1) is incident upon a glass plate (n = 1.3). It hits with an angle of incidence of 45°. If the angle of incidence increases to 50°, what is the new angle of refraction?
a. It is 45°
b. It is 50°
c. It is below 45°
d. It is above 50°

52. An object is placed a certain distance away from a convex spherical mirror. Which of the following statements is true?

    a. No image is formed.

    b. The image will be larger or smaller, depending on the object's distance from the mirror.

    c. The image will be smaller and right side up.

    d. The image will be smaller and either right side up or upside down, depending on the object's distance from the mirror.

Verbal Reasoning Practice Questions

Analogies

Directions: Choose the word that **best** completes the analogy in capital letters.

1. WHISPER : YELL :: TAP :
   a. water
   b. pat
   c. dance
   d. jab

2. EUCALYPTUS : TREE :: IRIS :
   a. tulip
   b. purple
   c. eye
   d. flower

3. IRKSOME : TEDIOUS :: INTRIGUING :
   a. fascinating
   b. silly
   c. unlikely
   d. impossible

4. PROGESTERONE : HORMONE :: BICEP :
   a. strength
   b. bone
   c. muscle
   d. arm

5. HOUSE : NEIGHBORHOOD :: TREE :
   a. leaf
   b. timber
   c. forest
   d. limb

6. WALLET : MONEY :: ENVELOPE :
   a. mail
   b. letter
   c. address
   d. post office

7. GERMAN SHEPHERD : DOG :: STRAWBERY :
   a. red
   b. vine
   c. seeds
   d. fruit

8. JOYFUL : SAD :: EMPTY :
   a. bare
   b. crowded
   c. productive
   d. vacant

9. AUTOMOBILE : GARAGE :: DISH :
   a. plate
   b. food
   c. cupboard
   d. spoon

10. DOCTOR : MEDICINE :: TEACHER :
   a. student
   b. teaching
   c. education
   d. school

11. CHIRP : TWEET :: JUMP :
   a. leap
   b. rope
   c. high
   d. street

12. SLEEPING : TIRED :: DRINKING :
   a. glass
   b. thirsty
   c. swallow
   d. water

13. FOUR-LEAF CLOVER : LUCK :: ARROW :
   a. bow
   b. Cupid
   c. shoot
   d. direction

14. QUESTION : ANSWER :: PROBLEM :
   a. mathematics
   b. solution
   c. worry
   d. trouble

15. SHOVEL : DIG :: SPOON :
   a. stir
   b. knife
   c. silverware
   d. eat

16. SHOOT : GUN :: DRIVE :
    a. road
    b. way
    c. automobile
    d. golf

17. SIMMER : BOIL :: TREMOR :
    a. earth
    b. earthquake
    c. shake
    d. nervous

18. INTELLIGENT : STUPID :: ENTHUSIASTIC :
    a. happy
    b. passionate
    c. action
    d. indifferent

19. BOUQUET : FLOWERS :: RECIPE :
    a. success
    b. cookbook
    c. ingredients
    d. chef

20. COOL : FREEZING :: WARM :
    a. boiling
    b. summer
    c. heat
    d. cozy

Sentence Completion

Directions: Choose the word or set of words for each blank that best fits the meaning of the sentence as a whole.

21. Marla used good judgment when she followed the advice of her ____ grandmother.
    a. capricious
    b. sagacious
    c. brusque
    d. obtuse

22. After being treated so badly by his grandson, Mr. Shepherd not only ____ him but also cut him out of the will.
    a. forgave
    b. edified
    c. inveigled
    d. repudiated

23. After getting into trouble yet again, Carline was not only _____ by the principal but also suspended for a week.
    a. castigated
    b. mollified
    c. abetted
    d. cajoled

24. Although he missed his old friends dearly and wished to be back in their good graces, Jerome understood that he had been _____ because of his _____ behavior.
    a. ostracized, egregious
    b. maligned, curious
    c. honored, charitable
    d. questioned, ambiguous

25. The teacher _____ her students when they gave the wrong answer.
    a. commended
    b. applauded
    c. belittled
    d. praised

26. Many rainforest species have _____ due to deforestation.
    a. perished
    b. persisted
    c. survived
    d. immigrated

27. Because of his easygoing _____, many people wanted to _____ James.
    a. personality .. destroy
    b. rudeness .. join
    c. demeanor .. befriend
    d. dominance .. ignore

28. Overcome with _____, the students built a monument to _____ their teacher after his death.
    a. melancholy .. memorialize
    b. sadness .. criticize
    c. blissfulness .. commemorate
    d. gratitude .. politicize

29. Her son's misbehavior _____ her, but she managed to calm down before she spoke to him.
    a. exhilarated
    b. depressed
    c. embroiled
    d. infuriated

30. The obstacles he faced seemed _____, but through hard work and _____ he was successful in his efforts.
    a. insuppressible .. retention
    b. mountainous .. indolence
    c. insurmountable .. diligence
    d. licentious .. persistence

31. Her goal is to _____ the globe in a hot air balloon.
    a. circumscribe
    b. circumnavigate
    c. circulate
    d. circumambulate

32. Paul made a bad decision to hike in _____ weather conditions.
    a. onerous
    b. affable
    c. malleable
    d. adverse

33. The teacher's lecture was so predictable, so _____, that the students fell asleep soon after it started.
    a. flippant
    b. banal
    c. inconceivable
    d. morbid

34. The mysterious, _____ music floated through the trees and charmed the listeners.
    a. ethereal
    b. viable
    c. polished
    d. nourishing

35. Rhonda's behavior only _____ an already bad situation.
    a. safeguarded
    b. pursued
    c. manifested
    d. exacerbated

36. Brian had a reputation for _____ trouble in high school, but he _____ after he started college.
    a. inciting .. deteriorated
    b. alleviating .. decreased
    c. instigating .. mellowed
    d. inferring .. oscillated

37. These birds are not _____ to North America; they were brought here by European immigrants.
    a. ingenuous
    b. fluent
    c. indigenous
    d. exigent

38. The varsity basketball team's perfect season _____ in a championship win over their biggest rival.
    a. culminated
    b. fumigated
    c. alleviated
    d. formulated

39. The jury _____ the mayor of all wrongdoing.
    a. expatriated
    b. exonerated
    c. augmented
    d. subjugated

40. A kind of _____ occurred when David graduated from high school; he suddenly became a serious student .
    a. accolade
    b. intrusion
    c. metamorphosis
    d. menace

Biological Sciences Practice Questions

1. The breakdown of a disaccharide releases energy which is stored as ATP. This is an example of a(n)
   a. Combination reaction
   b. Replacement reaction
   c. Endothermic reaction
   d. Exothermic reaction
   e. Thermodynamic reaction

2. Which of the following molecules is thought to have acted as the first enzyme in early life on earth?
   a. Protein
   b. RNA
   c. DNA
   d. Triglycerides
   e. Phospholipids

3. Cyanide is a poison that binds to the active site of the enzyme cytochrome c and prevents its activity. Cyanide is a(n)
   a. Prosthetic group
   b. Cofactor
   c. Coenzyme
   d. Inhibitor
   e. Reverse regulator

4. In photosynthesis, high-energy electrons move through electron transport chains to produce ATP and NADPH. Which of the following provides the energy to create high energy electrons?
   a. NADH
   b. NADP+
   c. O2
   d. Water
   e. Light

5. The synaptonemal complex is present in which of the following phases of the cell cycle?
   a. Metaphase of mitosis
   b. Metaphase of meiosis I
   c. Telophase of meiosis I
   d. Metaphase of meiosis II
   e. Telophase of meiosis II

6. Leaves have parallel veins
    a. Monocots
    b. Dicots
    c. Angiosperms
    d. Gymnosperms
    e. Nonvascular plants

7. In ferns, the joining of egg and sperm produces a zygote, which will grow into the
    a. Gametophyte
    b. Sporophyte
    c. Spore
    d. Sporangium
    e. Seedling

Questions 8 and 9 pertains to the following diagram of a complete, perfect flower

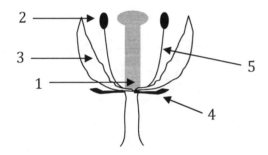

8. The structure in which microspores are produced.
    a. 1
    b. 2
    c. 3
    d. 4
    e. 5

9. The structures composed solely of diploid cells
    a. 1, 2, and 3
    b. 2, 3, and 4
    c. 3, 4, and 5
    d. 1, 4, and 5
    e. 1, 2, and 4

10. Which of the following processes is an example of positive feedback?
    a. High CO2 blood levels stimulate respiration which decreases blood CO2 levels
    b. High blood glucose levels stimulate insulin release, which makes muscle and liver cells take in glucose
    c. Increased nursing stimulates increased milk production in mammary glands
    d. Low blood oxygen levels stimulate erythropoietin production which increases red blood cell production by bone marrow
    e. Low blood calcium levels stimulate parathyroid hormone release from the parathyroid gland. Parathyroid hormone stimulates calcium release from bones.

11. In which of the following stages of embryo development are the three primary germ layers first present?
   a. Zygote
   b. Gastrula
   c. Morula
   d. Blastula
   e. Coelomate

12. In the food chain below, vultures represent:
$$grass \rightarrow cow \rightarrow wolf \rightarrow vulture$$
   a. Scavengers
   b. Detritivores
   c. Primary carnivores
   d. Herbivores
   e. Secondary consumers

13. A population of 1000 individuals has 110 births and 10 deaths in a year. Its growth rate (r) is equal to
   a. 0.01 per year
   b. 0.1 per year
   c. 0.09 per year
   d. 0.11 per year
   e. 0.009 per year

14. When a population reaches its carrying capacity
   a. Other populations will be forced out of the habitat
   b. Density-dependent factors no longer play a role
   c. Density-independent factors no longer play a role
   d. The population growth rate approaches zero
   e. The population size begins to decrease

15. Darwin's idea that evolution occurs by the gradual accumulation of small changes can be summarized as
   a. Punctuated equilibrium
   b. Phyletic gradualism
   c. Convergent evolution
   e. Adaptive radiation
   e. Sympatric speciation

16. Human predation has cause the population of cheetahs to decline dramatically. Changes in allele frequencies in the remaining population of cheetahs would most likely be due to
   a. Mutation
   b. The bottleneck effect
   c. The founder effect
   d. Gene flow
   e. Natural selection

17. Which of the following carbohydrate polymers serves as an energy storage molecule in plants?
    a. Chitin
    b. Cellulose
    c. Starch
    d. Glycogen
    e. Phospholipids

18. All of the following molecules are soluble in water except:
    a. Polysaccharides
    b. Hydroxyl groups
    c. Carboxylic acids
    d. Polypeptides
    e. Triglycerides

19. The diagram below depicts a metabolic pathway. When product D accumulates, the production of product C decreases, D is an inhibitor of which enzyme?

$$A \xrightarrow{A'} B \xrightarrow{B'} C \xrightarrow{C'} D \xrightarrow{D'} E \xrightarrow{E'} F$$
$$\searrow G$$

    a. A'
    b. B'
    c. C'
    d. D'
    e. E'

20. Which of the following is a characteristic of an enzyme cofactor?
    a. It binds to an enzyme's active site
    b. It is consumed in the enzymatic reaction
    c. It inhibits the enzymatic reaction
    d. It binds to an allosteric site
    e. It is covalently bound to the enzyme

21. In photosynthesis, high-energy electrons in Photosystem II are transferred along an electron transport chain and eventually end up in high-energy molecules used in the Calvin Cycle. Which molecule provides electrons to replace those lost by Photosystem II after light stimulation?
    a. NADPH
    b. H2O
    c. ATP
    d. CO2
    e. FADH2

22. Auxin stimulates stem elongation and is involved in the process of phototropism. If plants bend toward a light source, in which region of the plant is auxin most likely to be found?
    a. The sunny side of a stem
    b. The shaded side of a stem
    c. The top of a shoot
    d. The bottom of a shoot
    e. The top side of leaves

23. Which of the following organisms has a circulatory system in which blood circulates in an internal cavity called a hemocoel?
    a. Earthworms
    b. Cats
    c. Birds
    d. Centipedes
    e. Eels

24. In animals, consuming glucose causes insulin release from the pancreas, which causes the liver and muscles to take in glucose from the blood stream. This is an example of:
    a. Thermoregulation
    b. Circulatory feedback
    c. Positive feedback
    d. Negative feedback
    e. Receptor feedback

25. What will be the genotype of the gametes produced by a *Tt* individual?
    a. All T
    b. All t
    c. ½ T and ½ t
    d. All Tt
    e. ½ Tt and ½ *tT*

26. Hemophilia is a sex-linked trait. From which parent(s) did an affected boy inherit the trait?
    a. Only the father
    b. Only the mother
    c. Both the father and the mother
    d. The mother or the father but not both
    e. Impossible to tell

27. Which of the following is the major way in which nitrogen is assimilated into living things?
    a. Erosion from sediments
    b. Fixation by bacteria
    c. Respiration from the atmosphere
    d. Transpiration
    e. Absorption from soils

28. If a population's growth rate is zero, it has likely reached its
    a. Minimal viable population size
    b. Full range
    c. Carrying capacity
    d. Mature age structure
    e. Intrinsic growth rate

29. As a result of herbicide treatment, nearly an entire population of a grass possesses an herbicide-resistant gene. This is an example of:
    a. Stabilizing selection
    b. Directional selection
    c. Disruptive selection
    d. Sexual selection
    e. Artificial selection

30. A population of pea plants has 25% dwarf plants and 75% tall plants. The tall allele, T, is dominant to dwarf (t). What percentage of tall plants is heterozygous?
    a. 0.75
    b. 0.67
    c. 0.5
    d. 0.25
    e. 0.16

31. The absence of which of the following molecules in the earth's early atmosphere allowed chemical evolution to occur?
    a. CO2
    b. O2
    c. H2
    d. HCl
    e. S

32. The general formula for an alkane is
    a. C_nH_{2n}
    b. C_nH_{2n+2}
    c. $C_{2n}H_{2n+2}$
    d. $(CH_2)_n$

33. An unknown substance is found to have a sharp melting point, and therefore
    a. it is a pure compound
    b. it may be a pure compound
    c. it may be a eutectic mixture of compounds
    d. both b) and c) are true

34. The sp^3 orbital is a hybrid of
    a. three sp orbitals
    b. the $3s$ and a $3p$ orbital
    c. the s and three p orbitals of the same principal quantum level
    d. three p orbitals of one principal quantum level and the s orbital of the next

35. Propanol, propanal and propanone
   a. have equal molecular weights
   b. are not reactive compounds
   c. have a three-carbon molecular backbone
   d. none of the above

36. Carboxylic acids (R-COOH) and alcohols (R'-OH) undergo a condensation reaction to form
   a. esters and water
   b. ethers and water
   c. a diacid
   d. a lactone

37. When two high priority substituent groups are restricted to opposite sides of a molecule they are designated as
   a. Z- isomers
   b. E- isomers
   c. R- isomers
   d. d,l- isomers

38. An *sp²* carbon atom that can form an asymmetric *sp³* carbon atom is called
   a. prochiral
   b. delocalized
   c. stabilized
   d. a resonance structure

39. A molecule with two adjacent chiral centers that are enantiomeric is called
   a. a *meso-* structure
   b. a *d,l-* pair
   c. a racemate
   d. a lone pair

40. The carbonyl group is found
   a. only in ketones and carboxylic acid derivatives
   b. only in ketones and aldehydes
   c. only in aldehydes and amides
   d. in aldehydes, ketones, and carboxylic acid derivatives

41. The NMR spectrum of a compound shows a triplet near $\delta1.0$ and a related quartet near $\delta1.3$ with the integration ratio of 3:2. This indicates
   a. an isopropyl group is present in the molecule
   b. an ethyl group is present in the molecule
   c. the compound is an ethyl ester
   d. one or more identical ethyl groups are present in the molecule

42. Carbon-carbon double bonds can be converted to vicinal diols by reaction with
   a. $KMnO_4$ in cold methanol
   b. $KMnO_4$ in hot acid solution
   c. $KMnO_4$ in cold methanolic KOH solution
   d. $K_2Cr_2O_7$ in cold methanolic KOH solution

- 26 -

43. Colored impurities can often be removed from a compound during the recrystallization process by
    a. filtration
    b. addition of a cosolvent
    c. addition of activated charcoal powder
    d. chromatography

44. Which of the following pairs of compounds are carbohydrates?
    a. glucose and cellulose
    b. starch and caffeine
    c. levulose and gallic acid
    d. mannose and pyridine

45. A carbonyl compound with α protons can undergo
    a. racemization
    b. inversion
    c. keto-enol tautomerism
    d. conformational isomerism

46. A Friedel-Crafts reaction requires the presence of
    a. HCl and Cl_2
    b. $AlCl_3$ or $FeCl_3$
    c. a Lewis base
    d. benzene

47. The reaction of benzene with excess benzyl bromide and $AlCl_3$ produces
    a. diphenyl methane
    b. no reaction
    c. 1,2-diphenylethane
    d. biphenyl

48. Amides can be produced by reaction of acyl halides with
    a. 1º and 2º amines
    b. 1º and 3º amines
    c. 2º and 3º amines
    d. 1º, 2º and 3º amines

49. Phosphorus has typical oxidation states of
    a. -3 and -5
    b. +2 and +6
    c. +3 and +5
    d. +3 and -3

50. When a solution of 4-t-butylcyclohexanone is treated with two equivalents of a strong base, followed by addition of a two-fold excess of 1-bromobutane, then quenched with water the product is
   a. 2-butyl-4-t-butylcyclohexanone
   b. 2-butyl-4-t-butylcyclohexanol
   c. 2,6-dibutyl-4-t-butylcyclohexanone
   d. 2,6-dibutyl-4-t-butylcyclohexanol

51. The primary structure of a protein molecule is determined by
   a. the relative positions of amino acid residues according to bond angles
   b. the sequential order of amino acid residues in the molecule
   c. the folding of the molecule at specific amino acid residues in the molecular structure
   d. the geometry of cavities in the overall molecular structure

52. Birch reduction employs
   a. activated charcoal powder from birch wood
   b. sodium amide
   c. sodium metal dissolved in liquid ammonia
   d. sodium metal in refluxing THF

Answer Key and Explanations

Physical Sciences

1. D: Generally, the larger and heavier the molecule, the higher the melting point. Decreasing polarity will lower intermolecular attractions and lower the melting point. Long, linear molecules have a larger surface area, and therefore more opportunity to interact with other molecules, which increases the melting point.

2. D: Since there are twice as many molecules of hydrogen present vs. oxygen, the partial pressure of hydrogen will be greater. The mass of hydrogen will not be greater than the mass of oxygen present even though there are more moles of hydrogen, due to oxygen having a higher molecular weight. Each gas will occupy the same volume. Hydrogen and oxygen gas can coexist in the container without reacting to produce water. There is no indication given that a chemical reaction has occurred.

3. B: Plugging the data into the ideal gas law using the correct units gives the correct answer in atmospheres, which in this case is 2.4 atm. The equation is $P = nRT/V$. So we have $P = 1$ mol $(0.08206$ L atm/mol K$)(298$ K$)/10$ L. The R value is 0.08206 L atm/mol K when using L as the volume unit, and delivers the pressure in atm.

4. D: Both liquids and gases are fluids and therefore flow, but only gases are compressible. The molecules that make up a gas are very far apart, allowing the gas to be compressed into a smaller volume.

5. C: As the temperature drops to -5 °C, the water vapor condenses to a liquid, and then to a solid. The vapor pressure of a solid is much less than that of the corresponding gas. The argon is still a gas at -5 °C, so almost all the pressure in the cylinder is due to argon.

6. D: $AgNO_3$, $NaNO_3$ and $NaCl$ are all highly water soluble and would not precipitate under these conditions. All nitrate compounds and compounds containing Group I metals are soluble in water. $AgCl$ is essentially insoluble in water, and this is the precipitate observed.

7. B: Pure water boils at 100 °C. Water that has salts dissolved in it will boil at a slightly higher temperature, and will conduct electricity much better than pure water.

8. A: The weight % of the acetic acid is the mass of acetic acid divided by the mass of the acetic acid plus the water. So $50g/(50g + 200g) = 0.2$, or 20%. The mole fraction is the moles of acetic acid divided by the total number of moles of the solution. So 50 g of acetic acid (MW = 60) is $50g/60$ g/mol = 0.83 moles. 200 g of water = 11.11 moles. Therefore, 0.83 mol$/(0.83$ mol + 11.11 mol$) = 0.069$.

9. A: Since we have 1 liter of the solution, then 0.02 M represents 0.02 moles of methanol. The mass of methanol can then be found by 0.02mol x MW of CH_3OH (32) = 0.64 g. Molality is the moles of solute (methanol) divided by the number of kilograms of solvent, in this case, it is essentially 1 kg. This is assumed since the solvent is water and the density of water is 1 g/mL. So 0.02 mol/ 1 kg = 0.02 m.

10. C: Since each half life is 2 years, eight years would be 4 half lives. So the mass of material is halved 4 times. Therefore if we start with 1 kg, at two years we would have 0.5 kg, at four years we would have 0.25 kg, after 6 years we would have 0.12 kg, and after 8 years we would have 0.06 kg.

11. A: Nuclear reactions convert mass into energy ($E = mc^2$). The mass of products is always less than that of the starting materials since some mass is now energy.

12. C: Hund's rule states that electrons must populate empty orbitals of similar energy before pairing up. The Aufbau principle states that electrons must fill lower energy orbitals before filling higher energy orbitals. The Pauli exclusion principle states that no two electrons in the same atom can have the same four quantum numbers, and therefore, two electrons in the same orbital will have opposite spins.

13. A: NaCl is an ionic salt, and therefore the most polar. F_2 is nonpolar since the two atoms share the electrons in an equal and symmetrical manner. CH_3OH is an alcohol with a very polar O-H bond. CH_3CH_2Cl is also a polar molecule due to the unequal sharing of electrons between in the C-Cl bond.

14. D: The correct structure of ammonium sulfate is $(NH_4)_2SO_4$. Its molecular weight is 132. The masses of the elements in the compound are: nitrogen 28 (2 x 14), hydrogen 8 (1x8), sulfur 32 (32x1) and oxygen 64 (16x4). To find the percentage composition of each element, divide the element mass by the molecular weight of the compound and multiply by 100. So nitrogen is (28/132)x100 = 21%, hydrogen is (8/132)x100 = 6%, sulfur is (32/132)x100 = 24% and oxygen is (64/132)x100 = 48%.

15. D: 1 kg of heptane (MW 100) is equal to 10 moles of heptane. Since 8 moles of water is produced for every mole of heptane reacted, 80 moles of water must be produced. 80 moles of water (MW 18) equals 1440 g, or 1.4 kg.

16. B: Since the conversion of B to C is the slow step, this is the only one that determines the reaction rate law. Therefore, the rate law will be based on B, since it is the only reactant in producing C.

17. A: Lewis acids are compounds capable of accepting a lone pair of electrons. $AlCl_3$ is a very strong Lewis acid and can readily accept a pair of electrons due to Al only having 6 electrons instead of 8 in its outer shell. $FeCl_3$ is also a strong Lewis acid, though milder than $AlCl_3$. Sulfuric acid is a Bronsted-Lowry acid since it produces protons. PCl_3 is a Lewis base since the P can donate its lone pair of electrons to another species.

18. B: The K_a of acetic acid is determined from the pK_a, $K_a = 10^{-pka} = 1.75 \times 10^{-5}$. This is the equilibrium constant for the acetic acid dissociation, or $K_a = [H^+][CH_3COO^-]/[CH_3COOH]$. Using this equilibrium equation to solve for the $[H^+]$, the pH of the buffer can then be found. Solving for the $[H^+]$ concentration, we get $[H^+] = K_a \times [CH_3COOH]/CH_3COO^-]$, or $[H^+] = 1.75 \times 10^{-5} \times [0.1]/[0.2] = 8.75 \times 10^{-6}$. $pH = -\log[H^+] = 5.05$.

19. C: Cooling means heat is leaving the system, so it must be negative. We have 5.9 mol of ammonia cooling 75 °C, or 75 K. So 5.9 mol x -75 K x 35.1 J/(mol)(K) = -15.5 kJ.

20. C: The first is an alkyne, which contains a triple bond between carbon atoms. The second is a ketone and contains a carbon-oxygen double bond. The third is an alkene, which has a double bond between two carbon atoms. The fourth is an imide, which contains a double bond between two nitrogen atoms.

21. D: Combustion of coal releases significant amounts of Hg into the atmosphere. When the Hg settles into the water, it becomes methylated and concentrates in fish, making them toxic to eat.

22. D: When adding, the answer will have as many significant figures after the decimal point as the measurement with the fewest decimal places. The total mass (ignoring significant figure) is obtained by adding up all four measurements. This yields B, not A. But since the first and second masses are precise to only a hundredth of a gram, your answer can't be more precise than this. The number 35.5918, when rounded to two significant figures after the decimal point (to match your measurement of 23.04) is 35.59.

23. C: To add and subtract vectors algebraically, you add and subtract their components. To add vectors graphically, you shift the location of the vectors so that they are connected tail-to-tail. The resultant is a vector that starts at the tail of the first vector and ends at the tip of the second. To subtract vectors, however, you connect the vectors tail-to-tail, not tip to tail, starting with the vector that is not subtracted, and ending with the one that is. Think of this just like vector addition, except the vector that is subtracted (the one with the negative sign in front of it) switches directions.

24. C: This is a problem of free-fall in two-dimensions. A thrown ball without air resistance will only be subjected to one force, gravity. This causes a downward acceleration of exactly 9.8 m/s^2 on all objects, regardless of their size, speed or position. Note: since the ball was thrown directly upwards, the HORIZONTAL acceleration is 0 m/s^2 and the horizontal speed at all times is 0 m/s. B is wrong because the force of gravity is always pointed downward and never changes direction.

25. B: The newton is defined in terms of the fundamental units meters, kilograms, and seconds ($N = \text{kg} \times \text{m/s}^2$), so it is not a fundamental unit. II is a verbal statement of $F = ma$, Newton's second law, which is true. If $F = 0$ N, then the acceleration is 0 m/s^2. If the acceleration is 0 m/s^2, then the speed is 0 m/s or a nonzero constant. This is a nonverbal statement of Newton's first law, meaning Newton's first law can be derived from his second law. Newton's second law cannot be derived from the universal law of gravity.

26. C: The centripetal force pushes you in toward the center of the ring, not towards the wall. The centripetal force also causes the ring to push against you, which is why it might feel like you're being push outwards. This force also causes friction between your back and the wall, and that's why you don't fall when the floor is removed, assuming the frictional force is large enough to overcome gravity. As the speed of rotation increases, the force exerted by the wall on your body increases, so the frictional force between you and the wall increases. Answer B is correct—centripetal force does cause you to change direction—but it does not explain why you don't fall. Also note that "centrifugal force" is an illusion; because you feel the wall pushing against your back, you feel like you're being pushed outwards. In fact, you're being pulled inwards, but the wall is also being pulled inwards and is pushing against you. Finally, you are not weightless on a ride like this.

27. C: The question asks how much friction is needed to START the block moving, which means you need to calculate the force of static friction. If the question had asked about the force needed to KEEP the object moving at a constant speed, you would calculate the force of kinetic friction. Here, the force of static friction is equal to $\mu_{static} \times N$, where N is the Normal force. The normal force (N) on the plastic block is the weight of the block (mg) = 10 kg x 9.8 m/s² = 98 newtons. The force of static friction = 0.6 x 98N = 59 N. Answer B is the force of kinetic friction, once the block starts moving. (Note: molecular bonding and abrasion cause friction. When the surfaces are in motion the bonding is less strong, so the coefficient of kinetic friction is less than the coefficient of static friction. Therefore, more force is required to start the box moving than to keep it moving.)

28. B: The weight of the masses is determined from $W = mg$. In this case, there is a force to the left/down of 20 kg x 9.8 m/s² = 196 N, and a force to the right/down of 30 kg x 9.8 m/s² = 294 N. The net force is 98 N to the right/down. This force is moving both masses, however, which have a total mass of 50 kg. Using F = ma and solving for acceleration gives a = 98 N / 50 kg = 2 m/s².

29. B: The torque acting on an object is the force acting on the object (in this case, its weight = mg) times its distance from the pivot point. Here, the masses and the bar are balanced, so the net torque is 0 N × m. This means the clockwise torque is equal and opposite to the counter clockwise torque ($m_1 g d_1 = m_2 g d_2$). Dividing the distance in half would only add a factor of ½ to both sides of this equation. Since this affects both sides equally, the net torque is still zero when both distances are halved. C would be the correct answer if the mass of the bar was not zero.

30. D: Impulse is the change in an object's momentum (mv), which is in units of kg x m/s. An object's impulse can change, depending on the forces acting upon it. For a ball rolling down a hill, gravity provides a constant force, which causes the ball to accelerate. This creates an impulse that increases as the ball gets faster and faster. This impulse does not exist for a short time, but will continue as long as the ball is accelerating.

31. B: Using conservation of momentum, the original eastward momentum = 75 x 5 = 375 kg m/s and the northward momentum is 100 x 4 = 400 kg m/s. Afterwards, the two skaters have a combined mass of 175 kg. Using the Pythagorean theorem (for a right triangle w/ hypotenuse A, A² = B² + C²), their total momentum will be $\sqrt{(375^2 + 400^2)}$ = 548 KG M/S. Setting this equal to mv, 548 = (175) v, gives v = 3.1 m/s.

32. B: The work-energy theorem can be written $W = \Delta KE$. It is derived from Newton's second law ($F = ma$) by multiplying both sides by the distance the object moves. This work is the work done by a force on an object, and not the work done by an object. Work is only done by an object if that object exerts a force on another object, causing a change in its kinetic energy or position. The work done on an object MAY equal its potential energy, but only if that potential energy is converted into kinetic energy. In real-life cases, some energy is converted to heat, for example, so the change in potential energy does not equal the change in kinetic energy.

33. C: The initial gravitational potential energy of the ball is mgh, where h is the height above the ground. At the top of the loop, some of this energy will be converted into kinetic energy ($\frac{1}{2}mv_{top}^2$). Since its height is 2R at the top of the loop, it will have a potential energy

here of *mg(2R)*. Using the conservation of energy: *mgh = ½m v*$_{top}$*² + mg(2R)*. Additionally, in order to maintain a circular path, the centripetal force must equal the gravitational force at the top of the loop: $\frac{(m\ v_{top}^{2})}{R}$ *= mg*, which can be rewritten as *v*$_{top}$*² = gR*. Putting this into the energy equation, you find *mgh = ½ m(gR) + mg(2R)*. Dividing m and g from both sides of this equation shows that *h = ½R + 2R = $\frac{5}{2}$R*. Answers A, B and C represent choices that testess are likely to find if they do the math incorrectly.
PE = (1/2)kx²(spring)

34. B: The total energy of an isolated system is always conserved. However the mechanical energy may not be, since some mechanical energy could be converted into radiation (light) or heat (through friction). According to Einstein's famous equation $E = mc^2$, energy is (occasionally, like in nuclear reactions!) converted into mass, and vice versa, where c is the speed of light. This does not affect the conservation of energy law, however, since the mass is considered to have an energy equivalent. This equation does not tell anything about the mechanical energy of a particle; it just shows how much energy would be generated if the mass was converted directly into energy.

35. D: The phase of a wave changes as the wave moves. When measured in radians, the phase fluctuates between 0 and 2π radians. It is this fluctuating angle that allows two identical waves to be either in or out of phase, depending on whether their sinusoidal forms are matching or not when they cross. Answers A and B are meant to emulate the wave's amplitude and wavelength, both of which are measured in units of distance (meters, for example) and not radians.

36. C: Although the acceleration of a falling object is constant (9.8 m/s²), this is not true for a pendulum. The total force on a simple pendulum is the resultant of the force of gravity on the bob acting downward and the tension in the string. When the pendulum is at the bottom of its swing, the net force is zero (tension = weight), although the bob does have a velocity. At the top of its swing, when it's changing direction, the tension is least. Therefore, the net force is greatest here, too. The bob is stationary momentarily at its highest level. Since F = ma, a large force means that the acceleration here is highest, too.

37. A: The amplitude of waves that cross/interfere is the sum of the instantaneous height at the point the two waves cross. In this case, one wave is at its peak amplitude A. The other wave, in a trough, is at its minimum amplitude -A. Since these waves are at opposite heights, their sum = A + -A = 0. Had the waves both been peaking, the sum would be A + A = 2A. If they had both been at a minimum, the sum would be -2A.

38. C: If the waves are 500 Hz and 504 Hz, they will have 504 - 500 = 4 beats per second. By definition, this would have a frequency of 4 Hz. This would mean 0.25 seconds between beats.

39. B: The density of a homogeneous object, liquid, or gas is its mass divided by its volume or the ratio of its mass to its volume. Density is inversely proportional to the volume and directly proportional to the mass. The ratio of the density of A to the density of B is 5:4 or 5/4. Hence, the ratio of the volume of A to the volume of B is 4:5 or 4/5. Alternatively one could solve the equation $5V_A = 4V_B$.

40. C: The pressure of water at a depth h is given by $\rho g h$ where ρ is the density of water. Here P = (1000 kg/m³ x 9.8 m/s² x 14 m) = 1.37 x 10⁵ N/m². To find the force of the water on the window, multiply this pressure by the window's area. F = $\pi(1m)^2$ x 1.37 x 10⁵ N/m² = 4.3 x 10⁵ N/m².

41. D: Irrotational fluid flow consists of streamlines which describe the paths taken by the fluid elements. The streamlines don't have to be straight lines because the pipe may be curved. Answer B describes the conditions for steady flow. The image of a paddle wheel may be used to explain irrotational flow, but (1) the wheel will not turn in an irrotational fluid flow, and (2) this only works if the viscosity is zero. When there is viscosity, the speed of the fluid near the surface of the pipe is less than the speed of the fluid in the center of a pipe. Rotational flow includes vortex motion, whirlpools, and eddies.

42. B: As water freezes and becomes a solid, that heat leaves the water and the temperature of the water decreases. Water is a rare exception to the rule because it expands when it freezes. Most other substances contract when they freeze because the average distance between the atoms of the substance decreases. Water, on the other hand, forms a crystal lattice when it freezes, which causes the Hydrogen and Oxygen molecules to move slightly further away from each other due to the lattice's rigid structure. The coefficient of thermal expansion is always positive. Answer C just restates the phenomena and does not give an explanation. Answer D is true but does not explain the expansion of freezing water.

43. C: The electric field at a point in space is the force acting on a small positive test charge divided by the magnitude of the test charge. Its units are newtons per coulomb and it is a vector pointing in the direction of the force. The electric field produced by a charge distribution refers to the electric fields at each point in space. All the electric field vectors are tangent to electric field lines or electric lines of force. The electric field produced by a charge distribution can be represented by all the electric field vectors. Or, it can be represented by electric field lines. In this case, the stronger the electric field the closer together the electric field lines are. Arrows on the lines indicate the direction of the electric field. Answer D is incorrect because the field is being represented by electric field lines, not electric field vectors.

44. A: Since like charges repel and opposite charges attract, putting a dipole in an electric field would cause the dipole to orient so that its negative side will point towards the electric field's positive side. Since electric fields flow from positive towards negative, an electric field pointing from south to north could be caused by positive charges in the south and negative charges in the north. Consequently, the dipole will line up opposite to this, with the positive charge on the north side. Answer B is not correct because such an orientation would be unstable. The least disturbance would cause the dipole to flip 180°.

45. B: For a positively charged particle, you would used the right hand rule (RHR) to solve this. Since this is an electron, you can either use the left hand rule, or use the RHR and switch the direction of the inducted force. The RHR gives you the direction of a force exerted by a magnetic field on a magnetic field. Holding your right hand flat, the fingers point in the direction of the velocity of a positive charge, the palm points in the direction of the magnetic field, and the thumb points in the direction of the magnetic force. For a negative charge, the force is in the opposite direction, or downward in this case.

46. C: In a vacuum, the speed of light has nothing to do with its wavelength, frequency or color. It's a constant 3×10^8 m/s. When light travels through a medium other than a vacuum, such as glass or a prism, it slows down, and technically different colors of light travel at slightly different speeds. However, in most physics problems, you should treat all light as traveling at the same speed.

47. D: "Conventional current" -- as is typically used in physics and elsewhere -- is the flow of positive charges from the positive to negative sides of a battery. In reality, protons don't actually move through a wire. Negatively charged electrons move, so conventional current really reflects the effective positive charge that's created by electrons moving in the opposite direction. Normally, the wide side of the battery represents the positive side, so conventional current would start from the wide side and move around until it reached the narrow side of the battery. Here, the batteries aren't labeled with positive or negative. However, that doesn't matter, since the batteries are oriented in opposite directions. If they had the same exact voltage, no current would flow. However, if one battery has a higher voltage than the other, the higher voltage battery would dominate the direction of current flow. Since you don't know the voltage of the batteries, you cannot determine the direction of current flow.

48. B: Since the ammeter is connected in series, it will draw current and reduce the current in the resistor. However, ammeters have a very small resistance so as to draw as little current as possible. That way, measuring the current doesn't significantly affect the amount of current traveling through a circuit. Voltmeters, on the other hand, are connected in parallel and have a high resistance.

49. C: A capacitor connected to a battery with a small internal resistance will charge up very quickly because of the high current flow. Once the potential difference on the two plates becomes equal to the emf of the battery, the electrons will stop flowing from the positive plate to the negative plate and the capacitor will be fully charged up. Connecting the capacitor to a battery with a greater emf will cause the plates to acquire a greater charge. However, the charge is directly proportional to the voltage. The capacitance is the ratio of charge to voltage and depends only on the physical characteristics of the capacitor.

50. A: The maximum current is derived from Ohm's law. I = V / R = 40 V / 20 ohms = 2 amps. However, because this is an alternating current, the instantaneous current actually fluctuates between +2 amps and -2 amps. Electrons effectively move back and forth. This means the average current is 0 amps.

51. C: The angles of incidence and refraction are defined as the angle made by the rays with a line perpendicular to the surface. The angles of incidence and refraction are given by Snell's law: $n_1 \sin\theta_1 = n_2 \sin\theta_2$. In this case, because glass has a higher index of refraction (n) than air, the angle of refraction will be smaller than the angle of incidence. Increasing the angle of incidence by 5 degrees will increase the angle of refraction, but it will still be below the original 45°. Proving this with Snell's law: 1.0 x sin (50) = 1.3 sin(θ), so Sin(θ) = 0.59 and θ = 36°.

52. C: Convex is the opposite of concave. A convex mirror bulges outward like the outside of a sphere. They always produce a small image that is right side up. These images are always

virtual, also, meaning the image appears to lie behind the mirror. A convex mirror with an infinite radius of curvature is essentially a plane mirror.

Verbal Reasoning

1. D: This is an analogy of relative degree. A yell is a much louder version of a whisper, just as a jab is a much harder version of a tap.

2. D: This is an analogy indicating types, since a eucalyptus is one type of tree, and an iris is one type of flower.

3. A: In this analogy based on synonyms, *irksome* means about the same as *tedious,* just as *intriguing* means about the same as *fascinating.*

4. C: This is another "type" analogy. Progesterone is a type of hormone, and a bicep is a type of muscle.

5. A: A house is a part of the neighborhood and a tree is a part of the forest.

6. B: A wallet holds money and an envelope holds a letter.

7. D: A German shepherd is a type of dog and a strawberry is a type of fruit.

8. B: Joyful is an opposite of sad and empty is an opposite of crowded.

9. C: An automobile is stored in the garage and a dish is stored in a cupboard.

10. C: A doctor works in the field of medicine and a teacher works in the field of education.

11. A: Chirp is a similar action to tweet and jump is a similar action to leap.

12. B: Sleeping is a solution for being tired and drinking is a solution for being thirsty.

13. D: A four-leaf clover is a symbol of luck and an arrow is a symbol of direction.

14. B: A question requires an answer and a problem requires a solution.

15. A: A shovel is used to dig and a spoon is used to stir.

16. C: Shoot is an action done with a gun and drive is an action done with an automobile.

17. B: Simmer is a milder form of boil and tremor is a milder form of earthquake.

18. D: Intelligent is the opposite of stupid and enthusiastic is the opposite of indifferent.

19. C: A bouquet is made up of flowers and a recipe is made up of ingredients.

20. A: Cool is a mild temperature and freezing is extreme; warm is a mild temperature and boiling is extreme.

21. B: If Marla's grandmother is wise, Marla would be using good judgment to follow her advice. *Sagacious* means "wise," so this is the obvious answer. *Capricious* means "flighty and erratic," *brusque* means "abrupt in manner," and *obtuse* means "slow to understand," so all of these choices can be eliminated.

22. D: We know that Mr. Shepherd was angry enough with his grandson to cut him out of the will. This information helps us eliminate choice A, *forgave.* We can also eliminate choice B, *edified,* which means "enlightened." And *inveigled,* which means "enticed or tricked into doing something," makes no sense in the sentence. *Repudiated,* which means "disowned" or "refused to have anything to do with," is the only answer that makes sense.

23. A: *Castigated,* which means "rebuked severely," is the only word that makes sense in the sentence. *Mollified* means "soothed, appeased, or pacified." *Abetted* means "aided in wrong-doing." *Cajoled* means "coaxed with flattery."

24. A: Without the introductory clause, any of the choices would work. But the introductory clause tells us that Jerome is out of favor with his friends and misses them, which suggests that they have ostracized, or excluded, him because of his egregious, or remarkably bad, behavior.

25. C: "Wrong answer" is a clue that indicates a negative word. *Belittled* means to *criticize.* All the other answer choices have a positive connotation and, therefore, do not fit the intended meaning of the sentence.

26. A: *Deforestation* would have a negative effect on the rainforest: therefore, *perished* is the only word that makes sense in the context of the sentence.

27. C: "Easygoing" is the word clue here. Find the word that indicates a similar personality trait. Demeanor and personality work best here. If someone is *easygoing*, you most likely do not want to *destroy* them. *Befriend* works best in the second blank, making Choice C the correct answer.

28. A: Death is usually associated with sadness and grief, resulting in melancholy. Both choices A and B have words that seem to fit the first blank answer space. However, a monument is not built to criticize the deceased, but to memorialize or praise them. Therefore, Choice A is the best answer.

29. D: Misbehavior does not usually exhilarate or embroil (excite or involve). It can depress or infuriate those who observe it. Use the clue "calm down" to narrow the remaining choices down to the word *infuriate*. Generally, a person does not need to calm down when they are already depressed. *Infuriated* is the right word choice here.

30. C: An obstacle could be insuppressible, mountainous, or insurmountable, so any of these choices could fit the first blank. Choice D is incorrect because licentious doesn't fit the context of the first blank answer space. However, retention and indolence do not fit in the context of the second blank answer space, so they can be ruled out. Choice C is the best answer and makes the sentence meaningful

31. B: The goal is to go around the world in a hot air balloon. Circumscribe means to limit or restrict and does not fit the sentence meaning. Circulate means to distribute and makes no

- 38 -

sense in context. Circumambulate means to walk around but it is unlikely that anyone would "ambulate" around the world. Circumnavigate means to travel completely around, and reflects the sentence's intended meaning . Circumnavigate is the best answer.

32. D: "Bad decision" relates to the weather conditions. Adverse means unfavorable, and therefore makes Choice D the best answer. Affable is a word that means very agreeable or personable and doesn't work here. Onerous or burdensome is closer in meaning but not as relevant as the word adverse. Meanwhile, the weather is never malleable, that is, able to be shaped the way we want it.

33. B: "Predictable" is the clue. Banal means to be common place or predictable. It can also be boring, capable of putting the students to sleep.

34. A: Ethereal means to be light or spiritual. Ethereal music could be mysterious and float through the trees. Ethereal is often used to describe music that touches the soul, making that word the best choice.

35. D: We're looking for a word capable of making a bad situation worse. Exacerbate means to increase in severity. It is the only answer choice that makes sense and imparts meaning to the sentence.

36. C: Inciting and instigating both fit the first blank. However, deteriorating does not make sense in the second blank. Choice C is the best answer choice. The other answer choices make very little sense in the overall context of the sentence.

37. C: Indigenous means originating or occurring naturally in an area or environment. This answer choice makes the most sense in the sentence context, since the birds were not native and were brought from Europe

38. A: *Culminate* means to come to completion. The words "perfect season" and "championship win" allude to the happy ending of the basketball season. *Culminate* is the only word that fits.

39. B: "We're looking for a word that indicates that the mayor was free from guilt. Exonerated is the only word that fits in terms of meaning and is the best answer choice.

40. C: The sentence indicates that a positive change seemed to occur as David transitioned from high school to college. Metamorphosis is the only word choice which indicates that David changed.

Biological Sciences

1. D: An exothermic reaction releases energy, whereas an endothermic reaction requires energy. The breakdown of a chemical compound is an example of a decomposition reaction (AB → A + B.. A combination reaction (A + B →AB. is the reverse of a decomposition reaction, and a replacement (displacement) reaction is one where compound breaks apart and forms a new compound plus a free reactant (AB + C →AC + B or AB + CD → AD + CB.

2. B: Some RNA molecules in extant organisms have enzymatic activity; for example the formation of peptide bonds on ribosomes is catalyzed by an RNA molecule. This and other information has led scientists to believe that the most likely molecules to first demonstrate enzymatic activity were RNA molecules.

3. D: Enzyme inhibitors attach to an enzyme and block substrates from entering the active site, thereby preventing enzyme activity. As stated in the question, cyanide is a poison that irreversibly binds to an enzyme and blocks its active site, thus fitting the definition of an enzyme inhibitor.

4. E: Electrons trapped by the chlorophyll P680 molecule in photosystem II are energized by light. They are then transferred to electron acceptors in an electron transport chain.

5. C: The synaptonemal complex is the point of contact between homologous chromatids. It is formed when nonsister chromatids exchange genetic material through crossing over. Once meiosis I has completed, crossovers have resolved and the synaptonemal complex no longer exists. Rather, sister chromatids are held together at their centromeres prior to separation in anaphase II.

6. A: Monocots differ from dicots in that they have one cotyledon, or embryonic leaf in their embryos. They also have parallel veination, fibrous roots, petals in multiples of three, and a random arrangement of vascular bundles in their stems.

7. B: In ferns, the mature diploid plant is called a sporophyte. Sporophytes undergo meiosis to produce spores, which develop into gametophytes, which produce gametes.

8. B: Anthers produce microspores (the male gametophytes of flowering plants), which undergo meiosis to produce pollen grains.

9. C: In flowering plants, the anthers house the male gametophytes (which produce sperm) and the pistils house the female gametophytes (which produce eggs). Eggs and sperm are haploid. All other tissues are solely diploid.

10. C: In a positive feedback loop, an action intensifies a chain of events that, in turn, intensify the conditions that caused the action beyond normal limits. Nursing stimulates lactation, which promotes nursing. Contractions during childbirth, psychological hysteria, and sexual orgasm are all examples of positive feedback.

11. B: The gastrula is formed from the blastocyst, which contains a bilayered embryonic disc. One layer of this disc's inner cell mass further subdivides into the epiblast and the hypoblast, resulting in the three primary germ layers (endoderm, mesoderm, ectoderm).

12. A: Vultures eat carrion, or dead animals, so they are considered scavengers. Detritivores are heterotrophs that eat decomposing organic matter such as leaf litter. They are usually small.

13. B: The growth rate is equal to the difference between births and deaths divided by population size.

14. D: Within a habitat, there is a maximum number of individuals that can continue to thrive, known as the habitat's carrying capacity. When the population size approaches this number, population growth will stop.

15. B: Phyletic gradualism is the view that evolution occurs at a more or less constant rate. Contrary to this view, punctuated equilibrium holds that evolutionary history consists of long periods of stasis punctuated by geologically short periods of evolution. This theory predicts that there will be few fossils revealing intermediate stages of evolution, whereas phyletic gradualism views the lack of intermediate-stage fossils as a deficit in the fossil record that will resolve when enough specimens are collected.

16. B: The bottleneck effect occurs when populations undergo a dramatic decrease in size. It could be due to natural or artificial causes.

17. C: Plants have cellulose as the major structural component of their cell walls. However, plants store energy as starch, not cellulose. Starch is a polymer of α-glucose molecules, whereas cellulose is a polymer of β-glucose molecules. The different chemical bonds between glucose molecules in starch and cellulose make the difference in whether or not the polymer is digestible in plants and animals.

18. E: Triglycerides are hydrophobic. They consist of three fatty acids joined to a glycerol molecule, and because of their long hydrocarbon chains, they are not soluble in water.

19. B: This is an example of negative feedback, a process whereby an increase in an outcome causes a decrease or slowing in the pathways that led to the outcome.

20. A: A cofactor binds to the active site along with the substrate in order to catalyze an enzymatic reaction. Like the enzyme, it is not consumed by the reaction. Allosteric effectors bind to a second binding site on the enzyme, not the active site.

21. B: Water and carbon dioxide are the two essential consumable molecules in photosynthesis. First, water is split into oxygen, protons, and electrons, and then carbon dioxide is used in the Calvin cycle to create glucose. The electrons from splitting water are used in photosystem II, the protons are used to create NADPH, and oxygen is a waste product of the splitting of water.

22. B: Auxin is found in higher concentrations on the shaded side than the sunny side of a stem. More elongation on the shaded side causes the stem to bend toward the light.

23. D: Insects and most mollusks have open circulatory systems. Vertebrates, the phylum Annelida (earthworms), and some mollusks (squid and octopuses) have closed circulatory systems.

24. D: In negative feedback, when a pathway's output (increased blood glucose) exceeds normal limits, a mechanism is activated that reduces inputs to the pathway (reduction of blood glucose). Conditions are monitored by a control center, and when homeostasis returns, the corrective action is discontinued.

25. C: Gametes are haploid and have only one allele. Half the gametes from this individual will have the T allele and half will have the t allele.

26. B: Sex-linked, or X-linked, traits can only be transmitted to males through the mother.

27. B: Plants and animals cannot use inorganic nitrogen. It must be fixed, or reduced to ammonium, in order to enter a living ecosystem.

28. C: The carrying capacity is the maximum number of individuals a habitat can sustain, so when the population size reaches this number, growth will stop.

29. B: Selection that favors one extreme trait over all others is called directional selection. If directional selection continues for many generations, the population will end up with only one allele for that trait.

30. C: According to Hardy-Weinberg equilibrium, $p + q = 1$ and $p^2 + 2pq + q^2 = 1$. In this scenario, $q^2 = 0.25$, so $q = 0.5$. p must also be 0.5. $2pq$ is equal to $2(.5)(.5)$ or 0.5.

31. B: Simple molecules were able to form in the earth's early atmosphere because oxygen was absent. Oxygen is very reactive and it would have supplanted other molecules in chemical reactions if it were present.

32. B: The general molecular formula for alkanes is C_nH_{2n+2}. Each carbon atom requires two hydrogen atoms and there must be two additional hydrogen atoms to complete the required total number of bonds to the terminal sp^3 carbon atoms.

33. D: Pure compounds are characterized by having sharp melting points. Eutectic mixtures are also characterized by a distinct melting point associated with a specific combination of two or more different compounds. Thus a sharp melting point is not sufficient by itself to identify an unknown substance as a pure compound. Only b) and c) can be unequivocally true statements

34. C: Only the s and p orbitals of the same principal quantum level are sufficiently close in energy to combine and form the hybrid sp^3 orbitals. The sp orbital is a hybrid of the s orbital and one of the p orbitals of the same principal quantum level. Therefore, the $3s$ and one $3p$ orbital would form the $3sp$ hybrid orbital, not the sp^3 orbital.

35. C: Propanol is the alcohol $H_3CCH_2CH_2OH$, molecular weight = 60 g/mole. Propanal is the aldehyde, H_3CCH_2CHO, molecular weight = 58 g/mole.

Propanone is the ketone H_3CCOCH_3, commonly known as acetone, molecular weight = 58 g/mole. All three are readily reactive molecules, and all three structures are based on a backbone of three carbon atoms. Only answer c) is true.

36. A: Acids and alcohols react to form esters by the elimination of the components of the water molecule from the two. In this reaction, the –OH from the acid and the –H from the alcohol "condense" to form a molecule of HO-H, or H_2O.

37. B: The Z- designation stands for "zusammen" (German, "the same") and indicates that the two high priority substituents are located on the same side of the molecular structure relative to each other. The E- designation stands for "entgegen" (German, "opposite") and indicates that the high priority substituents are located on opposite sides of the molecular structure relative to each other.
The R- and d,l designations indicate the absolute configuration and the direction of optical rotation about an asymmetric sp^3 carbon atom.

38. A: An sp^2 carbon atom has three substituents in a trigonal planar geometry. The carbonium ion is a prime example. As a fourth substituent bond forms, the atom changes its hybridization from trigonal sp^2 to tetrahedral sp^3. The fourth bond can form on either face of the sp^2 arrangement to generate either a left-handed or right-handed tetrahedral arrangement of four different substituents. The three substituents on the sp^2 center must be different from each other and from the fourth substituent for this to be true. An sp^2 carbon atom that meets these requirements has the potential to form a chiral sp^3 center and is therefore referred to as prochiral.
"Delocalized" refers to the ability of electrons to move through adjacent p orbitals that are subject to sideways overlap.
"Stabilized" refers to the electronic influence exerted by substituents that imparts greater stability to a particular structure.
"Resonance structures" are equivalent arrangements of the bonds in a molecule.

39. A: The d,l- designation is not generally used since its meaning was deemed to be ambiguous. The term "racemate" is used when the mixture contains equal quantities of molecules that are individually mirror images of each other, or enantiomers. The term "lone pair" refers to a pair of valence electrons on an atom that are not involved in bonding. A meso- structure is a molecule in which two chiral centers exist across a plane of symmetry in enantiomeric configurations.

40. D: The carbonyl group is a characteristic feature common to all aldehydes, ketones and carboxylic acid derivatives. The carbonyl group is a carbon double bonded to an oxygen (C=O). Amides also contain a carbonyl group bonded to a N atom.

41. D: Proton signals in NMR exhibit "spin splitting" according to the number of different protons on adjacent carbon atoms. Protons experiencing identical magnetic environments produce identical signals, so the three protons of a single methyl group produce just one peak at about δ1.0. In an ethyl group, $-CH_2CH_3$, the three methyl protons are affected by the two $-CH_2-$ protons and their signal is split into three slightly different peaks called a "triplet". The $-CH_2-$ proton signal is split by the three $-CH_3$ protons into four slightly different peaks called a quartet. Integration of the quartet and the triplet sets of peaks is in the ratio of 2:3 respectively, according to the number of each different type of proton. There is certainly one ethyl group present indicated by this pattern, but it does not preclude the

- 43 -

possibility that there may be two or more identical ethyl groups in the molecule. They would still have a 2:3 integration ratio, so in this case the correct answer is d).

42. C: The permanganate ion coordinates to a C=C bond and subsequently transfers two O atoms to the alkene carbon atoms. The process requires base catalysis in methanol solution and produces a compound in which the two C=C carbon atoms each acquire an –OH group. Compounds with an –OH group on each of two adjacent carbon atoms are called "vicinal" diols.
The reaction does not occur in hot acid solution, or with potassium dichromate.

43. C: Activated charcoal powder acts as an adsorbent. The molecules of colored impurities tend to be polar compounds that adhere to the surfaces of the charcoal powder. Subsequently, filtration to remove the charcoal powder also removes the colored impurities.
Filtration alone can only remove impurities that are present as solids, colored or otherwise. A cosolvent is used in recrystallization either to form a suitable solvent system or to initiate the formation of crystals.
Chromatography is a procedure for separating compounds in a mixture and is not part of the recrystallization process.

44. A: Cellulose is a biopolymer, which is a large molecule produced by the sequential linking of hundreds and thousands of individual glucose molecules. Glucose is a "simple sugar", a single carbohydrate molecule, so its polymeric form, cellulose, is also a carbohydrate. The names of all carbohydrate molecules end in –ose. Starch is also a carbohydrate. It is similar to cellulose but composed of shorter polymeric chains of sequential glucose molecules.
Levulose, also known as fructose, and mannose are also carbohydrates. Mannose is an epimer of glucose. Epimers are diastereomers that have multiple stereocenters, but they differ in configuration at only one.
Caffeine is an alkaloid, not a carbohydrate.
Gallic acid is a carboxylic acid, not a carbohydrate.
Pyridine, C_5H_5N, is a six-membered ring nitrogen heterocycle analogous to benzene, C_6H_6, and is not a carbohydrate.

45. C: A carbonyl compound with α protons can rearrange to an equivalent form that is only slightly less stable than the carbonyl structure. This second form is called an enol, because it has an –OH group attached to a C=C bond. The two forms are called "tautomers" and the process of interconversion between the two forms is keto – enol tautomerism.
Racemization is the formation of an equal mixture of two enantiomers.
Inversion is the reversal of the relative orientation of three substituents about an sp^3 carbon atom in an S_N2 substitution reaction mechanism.
Conformational isomerism is the ability of a molecule to exist in different shapes, for example, the *chair* and *boat* conformations of cyclohexane.

46. B: Friedel-Crafts reactions typically use a strong Lewis acid such as $AlCl_3$ or $FeCl_3$ as a catalyst. Hydrogen chloride is not effective as a catalyst for Friedel-Crafts reactions. Friedel-Crafts reactions are applicable to most aryl and aromatic compounds.

47. A: This is a Friedel-Crafts alkylation reaction, in which the benzyl group, $C_6H_5CH_2-$, replaces an H atom on the benzene ring to form diphenylmethane, $C_6H_5CH_2C_6H_5$

48. A: Amides are formed by the replacement of an amine H atom by the acyl group of an acyl halide. Only amines with H atoms bonded to the amine N atom can undergo this reaction to produce an amide, so only primary and secondary amines can react in this way to produce amides.
Tertiary amines can accept the acyl halide to form an acyl trialkylammonium salt, but not an amide.

49. C: Phosphorus is in the same group as nitrogen and forms analogous compounds. It has oxidation states of +3 in compounds such as phosphines and +5 in compounds such as phosphine oxides and phosphates.

50. C: This is a nucleophilic substitution reaction. The base extracts an α proton from 4-t-butylcyclohexanone to generate an enolate anion. This then acts as a nucleophile to replace the bromine atom of 1-bromobutane. The reaction "alkylates" the 4-t-butylcyclohexanone molecule. The second equivalent of base allows the reaction to occur a second time, alkylating the cyclohexanone again on the opposite side of the carbonyl group.

51. B: Proteins are biopolymers of amino acids connected head-to-tail through peptide bonds (amide structures). The sequential order of the amino acids in the protein molecule is designated as the primary structure of the protein.

The folding of the molecule at specific amino acid locations is designated as the secondary structure of the protein molecule, and is due to the relative positions of the amino acids according to bond angles. This also determines the fundamental geometry of cavities and other features in the overall structure. Hydrogen bonding also plays an important role in the folding of the peptide chain in the secondary structure.

52. C: The initial step of a Birch reduction is the preparation of the Birch reducing agent by dissolving sodium metal in liquid ammonia. The intense blue color of the resulting solution is attributed to solvated electrons. Birch reduction is a very strong reduction method because the electrons act directly on the target molecule. The method readily reduces the benzene ring to a 1,4-cyclohexadiene system.

Birch reduction has nothing whatsoever to do with charcoal powder from birch wood. The active principle in Birch reduction is electrons dissolved in liquid ammonia from sodium metal. It is not sodium amide, $NaNH_2$, which is a very strong base.

Sodium metal in refluxing THF is a method of ensuring that the sodium contains no traces of dissolved water. That method is more effective when benzophenone, $C_6H_5COC_6H_5$, is added to the mixture, and a dark blue color is generated in the refluxing THF when benzophenone is present.

Practice Test #2

Physical Sciences Practice Questions

1. A gas at constant volume is cooled. Which statement about the gas must be true?
    a. The kinetic energy of the gas molecules has decreased.
    b. The gas has condensed to a liquid.
    c. The weight of the gas has decreased.
    d. The density of the gas has increased.

2. Graham's law is best used to determine what relationship between two different materials?
    a. pressure and volume
    b. volume and temperature
    c. mass and diffusion rate
    d. Diffusion rate and temperature

3. A 10 L cylinder contains 4 moles of oxygen, 3 moles of nitrogen and 7 moles of neon. The temperature of the cylinder is increased from 20 °C to 40 °C. Determine the partial pressure of neon in the cylinder as a percentage of the whole.
    a. 50%
    b. 70%
    c. 90%
    d. 40%

4. Which of the following statements **generally** describes the trend of electronegativity considering the Periodic Table of the Elements?
    a. Electronegativity increases going from left to right and from top to bottom
    b. Electronegativity increases going from right to left and from bottom to top
    c. Electronegativity increases going from left to right and from bottom to top
    d. Electronegativity increases going from right to left and from top to bottom

5. A solid is heated until it melts. Which of the following is true about the solid melting?
    a. ΔH is positive, and ΔS is positive
    b. ΔH is negative and ΔS is positive
    c. ΔH is positive and ΔS is negative
    d. ΔH is negative and ΔS is negative

6. 100 g of ethanol C_2H_6O is dissolved in 100 g of water. The final solution has a volume of 0.2 L. What is the density of the resulting solution?
    a. 0.5 g/mL
    b. 1 g/mL
    c. 46 g/mL
    d. 40 g/mL

7. Place the following in the correct order of increasing acidity.
    a. HCl<HF<HI<HBr
    b. HCl<HBr<HI<HF
    c. HI<HBr<HCl<HF
    d. HF<HCl<HBr<HI

8. Ammonium Phosphate $(NH_4)_3PO_4$ is a strong electrolyte. What will be the concentration of all the ions in a 0.9 M solution of ammonium phosphate?
    a. 0.9 M NH_4+, 0.9 M PO_4^{3-}
    b. 0.3 M NH_4+, 0.9 M PO_4^{3-}
    c. 2.7 M NH_4+, 0.9 M PO_4^{3-}
    d. 2.7 M NH_4^+, 2.7 M PO_4^{3-}

9. A 1 M solution of NaCl (A) and a 0.5 M solution of NaCl (B) are joined together by a semi permeable membrane. What, if anything, is likely to happen between the two solutions?
    a. No change, the solvents and solutes are the same in each
    b. Water will migrate from A to B
    c. NaCl will migrate from A to B and water will migrate from B to A.
    d. Water will migrate from B to A.

10. C-14 has a half life of 5730 years. If you started with 1 mg of C-14 today, how much would be left in 20,000 years?
    a. 0.06 mg
    b. 0.07 mg
    c. 0.11 mg
    d. 0.09 mg

11. Determine the number of neutrons, protons and electrons in ^{238}U.
    a. 238, 92, 238
    b. 92, 146, 146
    c. 146, 92, 92
    d. 92, 92, 146

12. Determine the oxidation states of each of the elements in $KMnO_4$:
    a. K^{+1}, Mn^{+7}, O^{-8}
    b. K^{-1}, Mn^{+7}, O^{-2}
    c. K^{+1}, Mn^{+3}, O^{-4}
    d. K^{+1}, Mn^{+7}, O^{-2}

13. Which of the following is an incorrect Lewis structure?

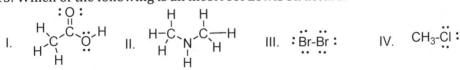

    a. I
    b. II
    c. III
    d. IV

14. What is the correct IUPAC name of the compound Fe_2O_3?
    a. Iron (I) oxide
    b. Iron (II) oxide
    c. Iron (III) oxide
    d. Iron (IV) oxide

15. Magnesium metal is reacted with hydrobromic acid according to the following equation:
    $$Mg + 2HBr \rightarrow MgBr_2 + H_2$$
If 100 g of Mg is reacted with 100 g of HBr, which statement about the reaction is true?
    a. Mg is the limiting reagent
    b. HBr is the excess reagent
    c. Mg is the excess reagent
    d. 100 g of $MgBr_2$ will be produced

16. For the gas phase reaction $CH_4 + 4Cl_2 \rightarrow CCl_4 + 4HCl$, what would be the equilibrium expression K_{eq} for this reaction?
    a. $[CH_4][Cl_2] / [CCl_4][4HCl]$
    b. $[CH_4][Cl_2] / [CCl_4][HCl]^4$
    c. $[4Cl][CCl_4\}/[CH_4][4HCl]$
    d. $[CCl_4][HCl]^4/ [CH_4][Cl_2]^4$

17. The pka for ethanol (CH_3CH_2OH) is approximately 16. The pka for acetic acid (CH_3COOH) is about 4. The difference can be explained by:
    a. Resonance stabilization
    b. Electronegativity differences
    c. Molecular weight differences
    d. Molecular size differences

18. 50 mL of 1 M H_2SO_4 is added to an aqueous solution containing 4 g of NaOH. What will the final pH of the resulting solution be?
    a. 5
    b. 6
    c. 7
    d. 9

19. Which of the following reactions produces products with higher entropy than the starting materials?
        I. Glucose (s) + water →glucose (aq)
        II. 4Al (s) + 3O_2(g)→2Al_2O_3(s)
        III. Br_2 + light→2 Br
        IV. Ice →water vapor
    a. II, III
    b. I, II
    c. I, III
    d. I, III, IV

20. Which of the following molecules is named correctly?

a.

methyl propionoate

b. OH

1-propanol

c.

3-propanoic acid

d.

3-butene

21. What would be the best analytical tool for determining the chemical structure of an organic compound?
   a. NMR
   b. HPLC
   c. IR
   d. Mass spec

22. Which of the following is a vector quantity?
   a. Distance
   b. Speed
   c. Velocity
   d. Time

23. A perfectly circular track has a circumference of 400 meters. A runner goes around the track in 100 seconds instead of her usual time of 80 seconds because a leg cramp causes her to stop running for 20 seconds. What is her average speed?
   a. 0 m/s
   b. 5 m/s
   c. 4 m/s
   d. 20 m/s

24. A space station is revolving in a circular orbit around Earth. Consider the following three statements:
I. The center of mass of the space station is necessarily located at its geometric center.
II. The center of mass is moving at a constant velocity.
III. The center of mass of the space station is moving at a constant speed.
Which of the following statements is true?
   a. I is true.
   b. II is true.
   c. III is true.
   d. I, II, and III are not true.

25. A box with a weight of 10 newtons is resting on a table. Which statement is true?
   a. The force of the table on the box is the reaction to the weight of the box.
   b. The force of the box on the table is the reaction to the weight of the box.
   c. A 10 newton force on Earth is the reaction force.
   d. There is no reaction force because the system is in equilibrium.

26. Bobsled tracks are flat when they are going straight, but when there is a turn, the track is angled (banked) to create a centripetal force. Assuming no friction, the banking angle is θ, the radius of curvature is r, and the maximum speed the bobsled can have without moving off the track is v. If the radius of curvature is doubled and the banking angle remains the same, which of the following statements is true?
   a. The maximum speed is $2v$.
   b. The maximum speed is $4v$.
   c. The maximum speed is $1.4v$.
   d. The maximum speed depends on the banking angle.

27. The diagram below shows a force F pulling a box up a ramp against the force of friction and the force of gravity. Which of the following diagrams correctly includes vectors representing the normal force, the force of gravity and the force of friction?

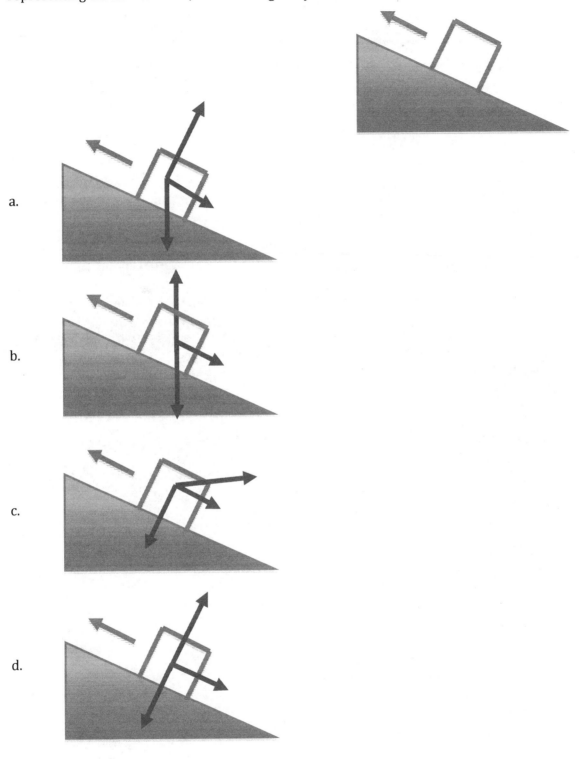

a.

b.

c.

d.

28. A force of 25.0 N pulls three blocks connected by a string on a frictionless surface. What is the tension in the rope between the 4.0-kg block and the 2.0-kg block?

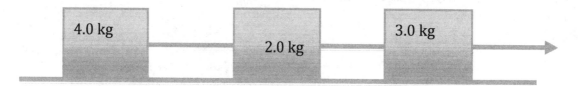

a. 0 N
b. 11.1 N
c. 16.7 N
d. 25 N

29. Suppose a moving railroad car collides with an identical stationary car and the two cars latch together. Ignoring friction, and assuming no deformation on impact, which of the following statements is true?
a. The speed of the first car decreases by half.
b. The collision is elastic.
c. The speed of the first car is doubled.
d. There is no determining the final speed because the collision was inelastic.

30. A teacher pulls a box across the floor at a uniform speed. He pulls it with a spring scale showing that the force of kinetic friction is 2 newtons. How much total work is done in moving the box 5 meters?
a. 0 joules
b. 0.4 joules
c. 10 joules
d. 20 joules

31. An athlete's foot is in contact with a kicked football for 100 milliseconds and exerts a force on the football over a distance of 20 centimeters. The force starts at 0 N and increases linearly to 2000 N for 50 milliseconds through a distance of 10 centimeters and then decreases linearly for 50 milliseconds through a distance of 10 centimeters. What is the average power of the athlete's foot while it is in contact with the ball?

a. 2 kilowatts
b. 4 kilowatts
c. 2000 kilowatts
d. 4000 kilowatts

32. Conservative forces are forces that do not lose energy to processes like friction and radiation and where the total mechanical energy is conserved. Which statement best explains why the work done by a conservative force on an object does not depend on the path the object takes?

    a. This is the definition of a conservative force.

    b. The work done by the force of friction on an object depends on the distance the object moves.

    c. Work can be positive, negative, or zero.

    d. If a force is conservative, any component of the force is equal to the change in a potential energy divided by the change in position.

33. A 100-kg bungee jumper jumps off a bridge, attached to a 20 meter bungee cord. After bouncing around for a minute he finally comes to rest. The stretched cord is now 25 meters long. What is the spring constant of the bungee cord?

    a. 20 newtons per meter

    b. 39 newtons per meter

    c. 49 newtons per meter

    d. 196 newtons per meter

34. A RADAR gun sends out a pulsed beam of microwave radiation to measure the speed of cars using the Doppler effect. The pulsed beam bounces off the moving car and returns to the RADAR gun. For a car that's moving away from the RADAR detector, which of the following statements about the pulsed beam are true?

I. It returns with a longer wavelength.

II. It returns with a shorter wavelength.

III. It returns with a higher frequency.

    a. I only.

    b. II only.

    c. I and III.

    d. II and III.

35. In resonance, small vibrations can produce a larger standing wave that becomes stronger than the original vibrations, assuming the vibrations are at the right frequency to generate resonance. If a pendulum is vibrated at a resonance frequency, what would you expect to happen?

    a. The period of the pendulum will increase.

    b. The time between swings will decrease.

    c. The pendulum will swing higher.

    d. The length of the pendulum will decrease.

36. In musical instruments with two open ends, the first harmonic fits one-half wave inside the tube. The second harmonic fits 1 full wave in the tube. The third harmonic fits 1.5 full waves in the tube. Etc. An organ pipe, open at both ends, has a length of 1.2 meters. What is the frequency of the third harmonic? The speed of sound is 340 meters per second.

    a. 142 Hz

    b. 284 Hz

    c. 425 Hz

    d. 568 Hz

37. A submarine sits underwater at a constant depth of 50 meters. Which of the following is true about the submarine's buoyant force?
    a. It is 0 N.
    b. It is greater than 0 N but less than the submarine's weight
    c. It is equal to the submarine's weight
    d. It is greater than the submarine's weight

38. Suppose you have a pipe of length L and radius r, and a liquid with viscosity η. You also have a sensor to detect the liquid's flow rate, which measures the volume of liquid passing through the pipe per second. If you want to increase the flow rate of the pipe, what changes to L, r and η should you make? Assume that the pressure differential remains constant.
    a. Increase L, increase r, and decreases η
    b. Decrease L, increase r, and decreases η
    c. Decrease L, increase r, and increase η
    d. Increase L, decrease r, and decreases η

39. A cube of aluminum is placed at the bottom of a deep ocean where the pressure is over 20 atmospheres. What happens to the density of the cube?
    a. It remains the same.
    b. It decreases slightly.
    c. It increases slightly.
    d. It becomes zero.

40. A cube of a substance is 5 centimeters on each side. It is placed in a pressure chamber where the pressure on each surface is $3.0 \times 10^7 \, N/m^2$, causing the density of the cube increases by 0.01 %. Which of the following theories is used to describe this?
    a. Young's Modulus
    b. Shear Modulus
    c. Elastic modulus
    d. Bulk Modulus

41. Which of the following statements about a solid metal sphere with a net charge is true?
    a. If the charge is positive it will be distributed uniformly throughout the sphere.
    b. The charge will be distributed uniformly at the surface of the sphere.
    c. The charge will leave the sphere.
    d. The electric field will be tangent to the surface of the sphere.

42. When is the potential of a point charge with respect to a dipole equal to 0 volts per coulomb?
    a. At the midpoint between the positive and negative charge.
    b. At an infinite distance from the dipole.
    c. At the negative charge.
    d. At the positive charge.

43. An electron is moving in a straight line. Another particle is moving in a straight line parallel to the path of the electron but in the opposite direction. Initially the electron and particle are far apart, but get closer together. When the two particles are in the vicinity of one another, they experience an attractive magnetic force. Which of the following is a correct inference from this fact?

    a. The particle has a north pole and a south pole.
    b. The particle is positively charged.
    c. The particle is negatively charged.
    d. The particle has either a north pole or a south pole.

44. Electromagnetic radiation — also known as light — consists of perpendicularly oscillating electric and magnetic fields. Which of the following statements about electromagnetic radiation is untrue?

    a. The energy of the radiation is determined by the frequency and Plank's constant.
    b. The "color" of light is determined by its wavelength.
    c. Electromagnetic radiation sometimes obeys wave theory.
    d. Electromagnetic radiation sometimes obeys particle theory.

45. Current in an electrical circuit is normally measured in amperes. Which of the following does not represent an alternative way of expressing units of current?

    a. coulombs per second
    b. volts per ohm
    c. electrons per second
    d. Watt-volts.

46. What is the total resistance between points X and Y in the circuit diagram below?

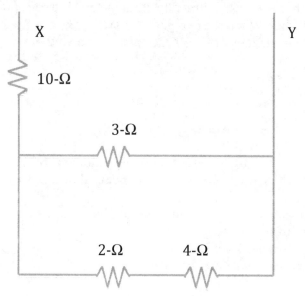

a. 0 Ω
b. 12 Ω
c. 19 Ω
d. 16 Ω

47. Which is the correct formula for the energy stored in a fully-charged capacitor with capacitance C when its attached to a battery of voltage V?
a. C/V
b. $\frac{1}{2}CV^2$
c. CV
d. 0 volt

48. A 6.0-megaohm resistor is connected in series with a 5.0-microfarad capacitor and fully charged with a 3-volt battery. The battery is disconnected and the capacitor is connected directly to the resistor. How long will it take for the capacitor to fully discharge?
a. Infinite time
b. 30 seconds
c. 0.0333 second
d. 90 seconds

49. Two beams of light with the same phase and wavelength travel different paths and arrive at the same point. If maximum constructive interference occurs at this point, which of the following statements is true?
a. The two beams arrive 180° out of phase.
b. The two beans arrive 90° out of phase.
c. The lengths of the paths differ by an odd-number of half wavelengths.
d. The lengths of the paths differ by an integral number of wavelengths.

50. Which of the following statements explains what causes a rainbow?
    a. The components of sunlight strike water droplets at different angles.
    b. Water moles produce an emission spectrum when sunlight strikes them.
    c. The speed of light in water depends on its wavelength.
    d. There is total internal reflection for certain wavelengths of sunlight.

51. An object is 20 cm centimeters in from of a thin convex lens with a focal point of 10 centimeters. Where is the image located?
    a. 10 cm in front of the lens.
    b. 20 cm in front of the lens.
    c. 10 cm behind the lens.
    d. 20 cm behind the lens.

52. Which type of aberration does not occur with concave spherical mirrors?
    a. Astigmatism
    b. Chromatic aberration
    c. Spherical aberration
    d. Distortion

Verbal Reasoning Practice Questions

Analogies

Directions: Choose the word that **best** completes the analogy in capital letters.

1. FRANCE : EUROPE :: CHINA :
    a. Japan
    b. Asia
    c. country
    d. continent

2. FABLE : STORY :: SANDAL :
    a. strap
    b. summer
    c. foot
    d. shoe

3. SHELL : BEACH :: ROCK :
    a. roll
    b. stone
    c. mountain
    d. dune

4. KITCHEN : COOK :: LIBRARY :
    a. peace
    b. read
    c. play
    d. pray

5. RUG : FLOOR :: SHEET :
    a. pillowcase
    b. bedspread
    c. sail
    d. bed

6. SMOKESTACK : FACTORY :: STEEPLE :
    a. church
    b. chase
    c. dome
    d. high

7. RAIN : WET :: FIRE :
    a. ash
    b. ember
    c. hot
    d. spark

8. SENTENCE : PARAGRAPH :: BRICK :
   a. mortar
   b. cement
   c. slate
   d. wall

9. TRY : ATTEMPT :: DARE :
   a. challenge
   b. devil
   c. fear
   d. defy

10. LAUGH : JOY :: SNEER :
    a. snicker
    b. snob
    c. contempt
    d.face

11. HOSPTIAL : SURGEON :: STORE :
    a. clerk
    b. inventory
    c. warehouse
    d. customer

12. WEAVE : BASKET :: KNIT :
    a. brow
    b. scarf
    c. sew
    d. needle

13. HUNGRY : EAT :: TIRED :
    a. bed
    b. awake
    c. sick
    d. sleep

14. DESERT : DUNE :: OCEAN :
    a. deep
    b. continent
    c. sea
    d. wave

15. OIL : SQUEAK :: SALVE :
    a. burn
    b. medicine
    c. soothe
    d. ointment

16. NUDGE : SHOVE :: NIBBLE :
     a. morsel
     b. devour
     c. tiny
     d. swallow

17. CAVITY : TOOTH :: WART :
     a. hog
     b. blemish
     c. skin
     d. virus

18. HAD : HAVE :: SAW :
     a. tool
     b. sawed
     c. see
     d. wood

19. RACKET : TENNIS :: PADDLE :
     a. hit
     b. punishment
     c. wheel
     d. ping pong

20. ETCH : GLASS :: PAINT :
     a. canvas
     b. draw
     c. color
     d. brush

Sentence Completion

Directions: Choose the word or set of words for each blank that best fits the meaning of the sentence as a whole.

21. Since Glenda was short of money, she decided that she would have to _____ the new appliances.
     a. foresee
     b. prohibit
     c. forgo
     d. suffice

22. The forecaster said that the high winds would _____ about midnight and that the next day would have light breezes.
     a. dispatch
     b. subside
     c. intensify
     d. capitulate

23. Since Gloria did not feel hungry, she looked at her dinner plate rather _____.
 a. ravenously
 b. voraciously
 c. indifferently
 d. gluttonously

24. Daniel attended an interesting educational _____ about _____ history.
 a. seminar .. maritime
 b. maneuver .. ancient
 c. conference .. malleable
 d. exterior .. conservation

25. He believed that in order to _____ the problem fully, he would need to understand all of its _____.
 a. solve...positions
 b. comprehend...extreme
 c. experience...thoughts
 d. embrace...nuances
 e. address...intricacies

26. The author's novel was _____ but she managed to develop numerous _____ fully and enjoyably by its end.
 a. thought-provoking...storylines
 b. brief...characters
 c. uninsightful...answers
 d. surprising...plots
 e. long-winded...chapters

27. The rumors were _____ and she welcomed the opportunity to _____ them.
 a. true...repudiate
 b. fabricated...correction
 c. believable...enjoy
 d. odious...refute
 e. pertinent...demystify

28. I was sorry to see her in that _____, she looked so _____.
 a. condition...despondent
 b. situation...arbitrary
 c. state...demure
 d. position...pensive
 e. mood...abstruse

29. The disarray was _____; the office had to be closed for the day so all the furniture could be placed where it belonged, papers could be re-filed and a general cleaning done.
 a. inconsequential
 b. contemptible
 c. severe
 d. intermittent
 e. trifling

30. He told the kids not to be so _____ when he was gone. He was afraid they would _____ the babysitter.
   a. placid...frighten
   b. boisterous...overwhelm
   c. obedient...enrage
   d. truculent...appease
   e. egotistical...endear

31. It was an _____ house with its vaulted ceilings, obviously expensive furniture and extravagant art covering the walls.
   a. off-kilter
   b. obstreperous
   c. odious
   d. obscure
   e. ostentatious

32. They chalked their meeting up to _____; it was the kind of lucky thing that could never have happened by design.
   a. preparation
   b. serendipity
   c. extravagance
   d. peculiarity
   e. concatenation

33. He was modest in his _____ and did not _____ a promotion to higher levels of responsibility at work.
   a. dreams...refuse
   b. failures...question
   c. habits...necessitate
   d. vision...challenge
   e. ambition...pursue

34. History did not feel _____ to her. Seeking a more _____ major she decided to study economics.
   a. relevant...topical
   b. important...literary
   c. familiar...theatrical
   d. esoteric...sycophantic
   e. important...trivial

35. She considered herself to be _____ and liked to predict events before they occurred.
   a. precocious
   b. prescient
   c. predated
   d. prefatory
   e. preferential

36. "If the yeti is _____", he asked, "then who made these _____ footprints?"
    a. genuine...invisible
    b. dangerous...massive
    c. imaginary...colossal
    d. welcoming...cavernous
    e. mysterious...unfathomable

37. Elijah noticed that the crowd had _____ and it was possible once again to walk around the museum _____.
    a. thickened...confidently
    b. intensified...on foot
    c. vanished...en masse
    d. dispersed...with ease
    e. startled...convincingly

38. The trip was very _____ and they vowed to each other that they would not take another for the _____ future.
    a. enjoyable...near
    b. unpleasant...so-called
    c. fruitful...distant
    d. dignified...immediate
    e. taxing...foreseeable

39. Because land is limited and the population is constantly growing, real estate _____ typically _____ over time.
    a. development ... falters
    b. values ... increase
    c. brokers ... compromise
    d. agents ... magnify
    e. properties ... classify

40. Infants and toddlers may sometimes have _____ sleep patterns due to growth spurts and rapid changes in their physical development.
    a. cohesive
    b. natural
    c. erratic
    d. fanciful
    e. mistaken

Biological Sciences Practice Questions

1. Which of the following metabolic compounds is composed of only carbon, oxygen, and hydrogen?
   a. Phospholipids
   b. Glycogen
   c. Peptides
   d. RNA
   e. Vitamins

2. Which of the following organelles is/are formed when the plasma membrane surrounds a particle outside of the cell?
   a. Golgi bodies
   b. Rough endoplasmic reticulum
   c. Lysosomes
   d. Secretory vesicles
   e. Endocytic vesicles

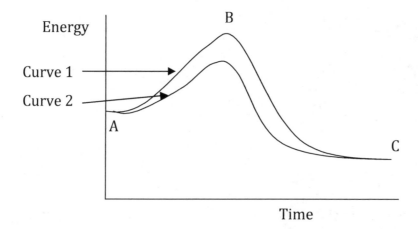

3. The graph above shows the potential energy of molecules during the process of a chemical reaction. All of the following may be true EXCEPT
   a. This is an endergonic reaction
   b. The activation energy in curve 2 is less than the activation energy in curve 1
   c. The energy of the products is less than the energy of the substrate
   d. Curve 2 shows the reaction in the presence of an enzyme
   e. The reaction required ATP

4. How many chromosomes does a human cell have after meiosis I?
   a. 92
   b. 46
   c. 23
   d. 22
   e. 12

5. A length of DNA coding for a particular protein is called a(n)
    a. Allele
    b. Genome
    c. Gene
    d. Transcript
    e. Codon

6. Produce seeds that are housed inside a fruit
    a. Monocots
    b. Dicots
    c. Angiosperms
    d. Gymnosperms
    e. Nonvascular plants

7. Which of the following is an example of the alternation of generations life cycle?
    a. Asexual reproduction of strawberries by runners
    b. Annual plants that live through a single growing season
    c. Ferns that have a large diploid and a diminutive haploid stage
    d. Insects that have distinct larval and adult stages
    e. Reptiles that have long periods of dormancy and metabolic inactivity

8. Animals exchange gases with the environment in all of the following ways EXCEPT
    a. Direct exchange through the skin
    b. Exchange through gills
    c. Stomata
    d. Tracheae
    e. Lungs

9. Which of the following blood components is involved in blood clotting?
    a. Red blood cells
    b. Platelets
    c. White blood cells
    d. Leukocytes
    e. Plasma

10. Which hormone is *not* secreted by a gland in the brain?
    a. Human chorionic gonadotropin (HCG)
    b. Gonadotropin releasing hormone (GnRH)
    c. Luteinizing hormone (LH)
    d. Follicle stimulating hormone (FSH)
    e. None of these

11. Which of the following is true of the gastrula?
    a. It is a solid ball of cells
    b. It has three germ layers
    c. It is an extraembryonic membrane
    d. It gives rise to the blastula
    e. It derives from the zona pellucida

12. Which of the following is the major way in which carbon is released into the environment?
    a. Transpiration
    b. Respiration
    c. Fixation
    d. Sedimentation
    e. Absorption

13. During primary succession, which species would most likely be a pioneer species?
    a. Lichens
    b. Fir trees
    c. Mosquitoes
    d. Dragonflies
    e. Mushrooms

14. Two species of finches are able to utilize the same food supply, but their beaks are different. They are able to coexist on an island because of
    a. Niche overlap
    b. Character displacement
    c. Resource partitioning
    d. Competitive exclusion
    e. Realized niches

15. Which of the following processes of speciation would most likely occur if a species of bird were introduced into a group of islands that were previously uninhabited by animals?
    a. Allopatric speciation
    b. Adaptive radiation
    c. Sympatric speciation
    d. Artificial speciation
    e. Hybridizing speciation

16. The first living cells on earth were most likely
    a. Heterotrophs
    b. Autotrophs
    c. Aerobic
    d. Eukaryotes
    e. Photosynthetic

17. Which of the following is not a function of protein in a cell?
    a. Encoding genetic information
    b. Storage of energy
    c. Structural support
    d. Transport of materials
    e. Catalysis of chemical reactions

18. Biochemical reactions take place in an enzyme's?
   a. Cofactor site
   b. Active site
   c. Prosthetic group
   d. Substrate complex
   e. Endothermic site

19. Cyanide is a poison that binds to the active site of the enzyme cytochrome c and prevents its activity. This kind of inhibition is called:
   a. Feedback inhibition
   b. Allosteric inhibition
   c. Competitive inhibition
   d. Noncompetitive inhibition
   e. Cooperativity

20. Which of the following is a characteristic of enzymes?
   a. They often catalyze more than one kind of reaction
   b. They are sensitive to denaturation by heat
   c. They catalyze reactions in only one direction
   d. They are primarily regulated by gene transcription
   e. They all require ATP

21. Which of the following photosynthetic reactions can only take place in the presence of light?
   a. Chemosmosis
   b. Photorespiration
   c. The Calvin Cycle
   d. Carbon fixation
   e. C4 photosynthesis

22. Which of the following would be most disruptive to the flowering time of a short-day plant?
   a. Daylight interrupted by a brief dark period
   b. Daylight interrupted by a long dark period
   c. High daytime temperatures
   d. Watering only at night
   e. Night interrupted by a brief exposure to red light

23. The digestion of starches begins in which part of the digestive system?
   a. The mouth
   b. The stomach
   c. The small intestine
   d. The large intestine
   e. The colon

24. Which of the following would NOT be an effective strategy for thermoregulation in a hot environment?
    a. Evaporation of water from the skin surface
    b. Restricting activity to nights
    c. Countercurrent exchange
    d. Increasing blood flow to extremities
    e. Muscle contraction

25. Two alleles of a gene will have the same
    a. Dominance
    b. Phenotypes
    c. Frequency in a population
    d. Locus
    e. Penetrance

26. In fruit flies, the traits for abdomen bristles and wing shape have several alleles but are always inherited together. This is an example of:
    a. Epistasis
    b. Pleiotropy
    c. Linkage
    d. Polygenic inheritance
    e. Incomplete dominance

27. Which of the following is the best example of a K-selected species?
    a. Grasses
    b. Mosquitoes
    c. Gorillas
    d. Mice
    e. Beetles

28. Which of the following is an example of a density-independent limiting factor?
    a. Sunlight for photosynthesis
    b. Food availability
    c. Predation
    d. Transmission of infectious diseases
    e. Pollution

29. Which of the following is *least* likely to cause a change in allele frequencies in a population?
    a. Mutation
    b. Random mating
    c. Immigration
    d. A rapid decrease in population size due to a natural disaster
    e. Inbreeding

30. Which of the following conditions would most likely lead to adaptive radiation?
    a. A mountain rising up and creating two separate populations of a species
    b. A plant becoming polyploid
    c. Hybridization between two species of flowers
    d. Inbreeding among a population
    e. Introduction of an animal onto a previously uncolonized island

31. Evidence that eukaryotic organelles evolved from prokaryotes includes all of the following EXCEPT:
    a. Mitochondria and chloroplasts have their own DNA
    b. Fossils of early endosymbionts
    c. Mitochondria and chloroplasts have two membranes
    d. Mitochondria and chloroplasts reproduce independently of the cell cycle
    e. Internal organelles are similar in size to prokaryotes

32. A compound with the molecular formula $C_6H_{14}O$ is
    a. an alcohol or an ether
    b. an aldehyde or a ketone
    c. an alcohol or an aldehyde
    d. an ether or a ketone

33. Which formula and structure are the same?

a. C_6H_6

c. C_6H_6

b. C_6H_6

d. C_6H_6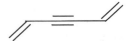

34. 1-Methylcyclohexene reacts with strong aqueous acid to produce
    a. no reaction occurs
    b. 1-methylcyclohexanol
    c. 2-methylcyclohexanol
    d. cyclohexylmethanol

35. A carbon atom and an oxygen atom double-bonded to each other is called
    a. a carbonyl group
    b. a carbonate group
    c. a carboxylic function
    d. an acyl group

36. Optical isomerism occurs in compounds that
    a. are enantiomeric
    b. are symmetric
    c. have multiple isomers
    d. have only one isomer

37. A molecular structure that is not superimposable with its mirror image isomer is called
    a. a geometric isomer
    b. a conformational isomer
    c. an enantiomeric isomer
    d. a structural isomer

38. Multiple bonds between atoms are characterized by
    a. shorter bond lengths and higher bond energies
    b. lower bond energies and shorter bond lengths
    c. decreased reactivity
    d. increased molecular weight

39. Chromatography is
    a. a method of separating and purifying compounds in a mixture
    b. an aid to identifying compounds in a mixture
    c. both a) and b) are true
    d. neither a) nor b) are true

40. The following molecule is

    a. a conjugated enone
    b. 2-phenyl-5-methylhept-4-en-2-one
    c. 2-cyclohexyl-2,5-dimethylhex-4-en-3-one
    d. known as caffeine

41. The IR spectrum of a compound has a strong, sharp absorption band at 1786 cm^{-1}, indicating the presence of
    a. a C=O bond
    b. a C$\equiv$N bond
    c. an ether C-O-C linkage
    d. a C=C bond

42. The reaction between a secondary alkyl bromide and hydroxide to produce a secondary alcohol normally proceeds via
    a. an S_N1 reaction mechanism
    b. an S_N2 reaction mechanism
    c. an E1 reaction mechanism
    d. an E2 reaction mechanism

43. Chromatography is a method of purifying compounds that depends on
    a. solubility
    b. absorption
    c. adsorption/desorption equilibria
    d. polarity

44. Six-carbon and five-carbon sugars
    a. have cyclic and acyclic forms
    b. are bicyclic
    c. cannot bond together
    d. cannot be recrystallized

45. When Mg metal is added to a solution of 1-bromopropane in diethyl ether
    a. a Grignard reaction takes place
    b. a Grignard reagent is formed
    c. no reaction occurs
    d. $MgBr_2$ is formed

46. The Grignard reaction between isobutyl magnesium bromide and cyclohexanone in anhydrous diethyl ether produces
    a. 1-(2-methylpropyl)-cyclohexanol
    b. cyclohexyl 2-methylpropyl ether
    c. 1-bromocyclohexanol
    d. cyclohexyl 2-methylpropanoate

47. The reaction of phenylacetyl chloride with toluene and ferric chloride produces
    a. p-(phenylacetyl)toluene
    b. phenylmethyl p-tolyl ketone
    c. 1-(2-phenylacetyl)-4-methyl benzene
    d. all of the above

48. The geometry of the amide functional group in amides is
    a. trigonal planar due to *p* orbital overlap
    b. tetrahedral at the N atom
    c. unaffected by the lone pair orbital on the N atom
    d. subject to free rotation about the C-N bond

49. The Wittig reaction involves
    a. addition of a phosphine to an imine
    b. addition of a phosphinium ylide to a carbonyl group
    c. addition of a phosphine oxide to a carbonyl group
    d. none of the above

50. The Williamson synthesis can be used to produce
    a. alcohols from ethers
    b. ethers from alcohols
    c. furanose saccharides from alcohols
    d. cyclic amines from alcohols

51. The steroid nucleus is

a.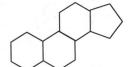

c.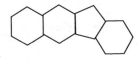

b.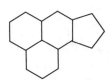

d.

52. A reaction in which two additional ring structures are added to a substrate molecule in the same reaction is called
   a. an annulation reaction
   b. a bicycloannulation reaction
   c. a double addition reaction
   d. a coordination reaction

Answer Key and Explanations

Physical Sciences

1. A: The kinetic energy of the gas molecules is directly proportional to the temperature. If the temperature decreases, so does the molecular motion. A decrease in temperature will not necessarily mean a gas condenses to a liquid. Neither the mass nor the density is impacted, as no material was added or removed, and the volume remained the same.

2. C: Graham's law of diffusion allows one to calculate the relative diffusion rate between two different gases based on their masses.

3. A: Since there are 7 moles of neon out of a total of 14 moles of gas in the cylinder, the partial pressure of neon will always be 50% of the total pressure, regardless of the temperature.

4. C: The most electronegative atoms are found near the top right of the periodic table. Fluorine has a high electronegativity, while Francium, located at the bottom left on the table, has a low electrongativity.

5. A: Heat is absorbed by the solid during melting, therefore ΔH is positive. Going from a solid to a liquid greatly increases the freedom of the particles, therefore increasing the entropy, so ΔS is also positive.

6. B: Density is determined by dividing the mass of the solution by its volume. The mass is 200 g, and the total volume is 0.2 L, or 200 mL. So 200 g/200 mL = 1 g/mL.

7. D: Acidity increases as we travel down the periodic table with regard to the halogens. Even though fluorine is the most electronegative element and would be expected to stabilize a negative charge well, it is such a small atom that it is poorly able to stabilize the negative charge and therefore will have a stronger bond to the hydrogen. As the atoms get larger, moving from fluorine to iodine, the ability to stabilize a negative charge becomes greater and the bond with the hydrogen is weaker. A stronger bond with the between the halogen and the hydrogen will result in less acidity, since fewer hydrogen ions will be produced.

8. C: Since there are three moles of NH_4^+ per mole of salt and 1 mole of PO_4^{3-} per mole of salt, the total ionic concentrations must be 2.7 M of NH_4^+, and 0.9 M of PO_4^{3-}.

9. D: During osmosis, solvent flows from the lowest to the highest concentration of solute, in this case B to A. The membrane is semi-permeable and only allows the solvent to move, not the solute.

10. D: Using the decay formula, C-14 remaining = C-14 initial(0.5) $^{t/t\ half\text{-}life}$. So, 1 mg (0.5) $^{20000/5730}$ = 0.09 mg. This problem is best solved using the decay formula since 20,000 years is 3.5 half lives. If a student is careful in their reasoning, this problem can be solved without the decay formula. After 3 half-lives, there would be 0.125 mg remaining. If allowed to

- 73 -

decay for 4 half-lives, 0.0625 mg would remain. Since only half of this half-life were allowed to elapse, only half of the material would decay, which would be 0.03 mg. Subtracting this amount from 0.125 mg, the amount remaining after 3 half-lives, gives 0.09 mg, which is the amount of material remaining after 3.5 half-lives.

11. C: The mass number is the number of protons and the number of neutrons added together. The number of protons is also known as the atomic number and can be found on the periodic table. Therefore, the number of neutrons is the mass number (238) less the number of protons, in this case, 92, so we have 146 neutrons. The number of electrons always equals the number of protons in a neutral atom, so C is the correct answer.

12. D: Each oxygen has a charge of -2 for a total negative charge of -8. Potassium (K) only exists in compounds as +1. Therefore for the molecule to have a neutral charge, the Mn must be in a +7 oxidation state.

13. B: The nitrogen is missing its lone pair of electrons, and should have two dots above it. A correct Lewis structure shows how the atoms are connected to each other as well as all of the valence electrons in the compound. Each bond represents two electrons.

14. C: Three oxygen are equal to a total charge of -6. Therefore, the two iron atoms must equal that with a positive charge, or +6. So each iron atom must be +3, and the compound is iron (III) oxide.

15. C: 100 g of HBr equals 1.23 moles, and 100 g of Mg equals 4.11 moles. From the coefficients of the balanced equation, the ratio of HBr to Mg is 2:1. This means that to react 1.23 moles of HBr, 2.46 moles of Mg would be required. Since 4.11 moles of Mg are present, Mg is in excess.

16. D: For a general reaction, a A + b B→ c C + d D, the equilibrium equation would take the form:

$$K_{eq} = \frac{[C]^c[D]^d}{[A]^a[B]^b}$$

where a, b, c and d are the coefficients from the balanced chemical reaction. Pure liquids and solids are excluded from the equation. Since all reactants and products in the problem are gaseous, the equilibrium equation for the reaction would be:

$$K_{eq} = \frac{[CCl_4][HCl]^4}{[CH_4][Cl_2]^4}$$

17. A: First, one must understand that pK_a is the acidity dissociation number. The larger the number, the less acidic. Acetic acid is a carboxylic acid. When H^+ is given off, a negative charge results on the O. Because there is a second equivalent oxygen bonded to the same carbon, this negative charge can be shared between both oxygen atoms. This is known as resonance stabilization and this conjugate base will be more stable and more of the acid molecules will remain dissociated resulting in higher acidity. For ethanol, when the O-H bond breaks, the negative charge resides completely on the O. It cannot be stabilized by

- 74 -

other atoms and therefore reforms the methanol rapidly. This results in very low acidity, since very few protons will be released.

18. C: There are 0.05 mol of sulfuric acid being added, but a total of 0.10 mol of H^+ since sulfuric acid is diprotic (H_2SO_4). This is being added to 0.1 mol of NaOH. The moles of acid and base exactly cancel each other out; therefore the pH of the resulting aqueous solution will be near 7.

19. D: In I, dissolving a solid into a liquid breaks up the organized solid matrix, therefore increasing disorder. III converts single particles into two particles, and in IV, solid ice sublimes into a gas. Both of these processes also increase disorder and thus, entropy. II is a decrease in entropy, since 7 molecules, with 3 being gaseous, are reacted to form 2 solid molecules.

20. A: B is 1-butanol, since its longest chain of carbons is 4, not 3. C is 3-pentanone, since there are 5 carbons in the chain and it is a ketone, rather than a carboxylic acid. D is 1-butene, not 3-butene. The name should be assigned by giving the double bond the lowest number.

21. A: NMR, or nuclear magnetic resonance, allows one to determine the connectivity of atoms in an organic molecule, by "reading" the resonance signals from the attached hydrogen atoms. IR, or infrared spectroscopy, can help to identify the functional groups that are present, but does not give much information about its position in the molecule. Mass spectrometry breaks apart a large molecule and analyzes the masses of the fragments. It can be useful in analyzing protein structure. HPLC, or high performance liquid chromatography, is a method used to separate a mixture into its components.

22. A: Vectors have a magnitude (e.g., 5 meters/second) and direction (e.g., towards north). Of the choice listed, only velocity has a direction. (35 m/s north, for example). Speed, distance and time are all quantities that have a size but not a direction. That's why, for example, a car's speedometer reads 35 miles/hour, but does not indicate your direction of travel.

23. C: The average speed is the total distance (400 m) divided by the total time spent travelling (100 s). Answer A would be correct if the question asked for the instantaneous velocity while the runner was stopped. Ans. B is the runner's average speed when running at her usual time, finishing the race in 80 seconds. Answer C is the average speed if the runner had completed the race in 20 seconds, not 100.

24. C: In a uniform gravitational field, such as occurs near Earth's surface, an object will move like a point mass located at the center of mass. However, this does not necessarily mean that the geometrical center of an object is the same as its center of mass, depending on its shape, design and mass distribution. The center of mass of a sphere or cube is at its geometric center because you can imagine the sphere as consisting of a large number of point masses located at certain points in space. Multiplying the point masses by their location and dividing by the total mass gives the center of mass. I is not true because the space station may not be completely symmetrical. III is true because the space station is undergoing uniform circular motion around Earth. If the orbit had been elliptical, this would not be true because the speed would have changed depending on the station's position. However, even though the speed is constant in a circular orbit, the velocity is not. Since

- 75 -

velocity has a direction associated with it, and the space station is moving in a circular path, its velocity is constantly changing.

25. A: Newton's third law is that if object A exerts a force on object B, then object B exerts and equal and opposite force on object A. This means for every action (force) there is a reaction (force in opposite direction). The box is in equilibrium because the force of the table on the box is equal and opposite to the force of gravity (weight) of the box pushing against the table. Since the force of the box against the table is an action force (caused by gravity), the reaction force would be the table pushing back against the box.

26. C: Centripetal force can be expressed as $F = m(v^2/r)\cos\theta$. Increasing the radius effectively decreases the force unless you also increase the velocity. By assuming that the maximum centripetal force remains constant, you can increase the maximum speed v by as much as $\sqrt{2}$. Any higher and the v^2 term will be too high for the new radius.

27. A: The force of gravity points straight down. The normal force is perpendicular to the surface of the block. The force of friction points down the slope. The only one of these diagrams with all three vectors pointing in those directions is Answer A.

28. B: Using Newton's second law $F = ma$, the acceleration of all three blocks, which have a combined mass of 9 kg, is a = 25 N / 9 kg = 2.78 m/s^2. The force pulling the rear block is F = ma = 4 kg x 2.78 m/s^2 = 11.1 N. Another way of thinking of this is the tension represents 4/9 of the total force, since the total mass is 9 kg and the rear block has a mass of 4 kg. This must equal the tension on the rope pulling on that block. Answer C is the tension of the string connecting the 3 kg and 2 kg masses. Answer D is the tension on the rope pulling all 3 masses.

29. A: A collision is considered elastic when neither object loses any kinetic energy. Since the cars latch together, this can't be the case. You could easily prove this by calculating the cars' KE = $\frac{1}{2}mv^2$. If the railroad cars had bumpers instead of couplers, the moving car would stop and transfer all its momentum and kinetic energy to the stationary car, causing an elastic collision. In a closed system like this one, however, the conservation of momentum is an absolute law, where an objects' momentum is its mass times its velocity. There are no external forces acting on the two cars. The only forces are between the two cars themselves. The momentum before the collision is the same as the momentum after the collision: $mv_{initial} + m(0$ m/s$) = mv_{final} + mv_{final}$. So $mv_{initial} = 2mv_{final}$, and $v_{initial} = 2v_{final}$. Thus the final velocity is half the initial velocity.

30. A: Since the box is moving at a uniform speed, the net force on the box is 0 newtons. Thus the work (W = Fd) is also 0 joules. Answer C incorrectly assumes that 2 newtons of force are used to move the box 5 meters, and while it's true that the teacher is pulling with 2 newtons, the frictional force counteracts this. Answer D incorrectly assumes the work performed by the teacher and the work due to friction add together for a net work of 20 newtons. Answer B incorrectly uses W = F/d. The vertical forces acting on the box—gravity and the normal force—also have a net force of 0 newtons and work of 0 joules.

31. B: In addition to understanding power, this problem requires you to understand unit conversions. The power P is the work divided by the time, and the work here is the average force times distance. Since the force increases evenly from 0 to 2000N and decreases at the same rate, the average force is 1000N. Keeping in mind that 20 cm = 0.2 m and 100

milliseconds = 0.1 seconds, this means P = 1000N x 0.2 m / 0.1 s = 2000 watts or 2 kilowatts.

32. D: Answers A, B, and C all shed light on what conservative forces are but do not answer the question of why the work on an object doesn't depend on its path. Friction is a force that causes kinetic energy to be lost and where the amount of loss depends on the path taken. Work can be expressed in multiple ways, including as the sum of potentials, and all that matters is the beginning and ending position. Think of this in terms of gravity, gravitational potential energy, and the work done by gravity. In this case, $W = \Delta PE = mg\Delta h$, where h is an objects height. Dividing work by the change in position shows $mg = \Delta PE/\Delta h$. Since mg is a force, you can say $F = \Delta PE/\Delta h$, or the force equals the work/change in potential energy divided by its change in position.

33. D: The jumper's weight is 9.8 m/s² x 100 kg= 980 Newtons. Insert the weight—a force—into the equation F = kx, where k is the spring constant and x is the displacement from rest of the spring. The displacement here is 5 meters. 20 meters is unnecessary information, and just a measure of how long the spring is, not how far it was displaced. k = F/x = 980 N / 5 meters = 196 N/m.

34. A: The Doppler effect shows that light/radiation from a object moving away has a longer wavelength. A car moving towards the RADAR gun would have a shorter wavelength. Since c = vf (where c = speed of light, v = wavelength and f = frequency), increasing the wavelength would cause the frequency to become smaller.

35. C: As the amplitude of the pendulum increases due to resonance, it will swing higher. However, the period of a pendulum is not connected to how high it swings. Only the length of the pendulum affects its period. Obviously, the length of a pendulum will not be affected by how high it's swinging or whether it's in resonance.

36. C: Three full waves fit into the pipe, according to the question description. The wavelength of the third harmonic in this pipe organ is 1.2m/1.5 waves = 0.8 m. Using the wave equation ($v = \lambda f$), f = 340 m/s / 0.8 m = 425 Hz.

37. C: If the sub stays at a constant depth, its buoyant force must be equal to its weight. If the buoyant force was larger, it would rise. If lower, it would sink. All objects underwater experience a buoyant force, so it cannot be zero.

38. B: To increase the flow rate, you'd want to: (1) reduce the length L of the pipe, (2) make the pipe wider, and (3) have a fluid with low viscosity (just think of how much slower a viscous fluid like molasses runs as compared to water). Answer B is the only answer that describes all of these changes.

39. C: In a vacuum the only forces acting on the molecules of aluminum are other aluminum molecules. Inside a fluid, the molecules of the fluid collide with the sides of cube and exert a force on the surface causing the cube to shrink in size slightly. Also, the temperature of water deep in the ocean is very low. This causes the vibratory motion of the aluminum molecules to decrease, which decreases the dimensions of the cube.

40. D: The bulk modulus describes a substance's reaction to being squeezed and its change in volume, which directly affects its density. The elastic modulus is the ratio of stress to strain for an object. Young's modulus deals with the elasticity and length of an object. The shear modulus deals with the elasticity of a shape and the stress that's applied perpendicular to its surfaces.

41. B: Concerning answer A, if an object has a positive charge, it is because electrons were removed. In the case of a conductor, the electrons will migrate away from the surface, leaving a positive charge on the surface. The electric field of a negative point charge points towards the charge. The electric field of a sheet of charges will be perpendicular to the sheet.

42. B: The electric potential, which comes from the electrostatic potential energy, is the potential of a charged particle in an electrical field. The stronger the field or the higher the charge, the higher the potential. So putting a point charge near a dipole will create a potential, depending on how strong the dipole's field is. For a potential of 0, you would need to be far from the dipole, so its electric field strength was effectively 0. At an infinite distance from a dipole, the distance between the charges is approximately 0 meters, so the net charge is 0 coulombs.

43. B: A moving electron produces a circular magnetic field that is perpendicular to the velocity of the particle. Since the magnetic field produced by the electron exerts a magnetic force towards the electron, the charge on the particle is positive. This conclusion requires the correct application of the right-hand rule for the creation of a magnetic field by a current (thumb in the direction of the velocity of a positive charge with fingers curling in the direction of the magnetic field) and the right-hand rule for the magnetic force on a moving charge (fingers in the direction of the positively charged particle's velocity, thumb in the direction of the magnetic force, and palm in the direction of the magnetic field). Answer D is wrong because there are no particles with only a north pole or a south pole. There may be a force between the electron and the particle if the particle is a tiny magnet, but the direction of the force would depend on the magnet's orientation, and hence answer A is wrong.

44. B: Although the wavelength of light is related to its color, the frequency really determines light's color. For example, light slows down when it enters water. This doesn't change the frequency or the color of light, but it does change its wavelength. The fact that light sometimes acts like a wave and sometimes acts like particles is called "duality." The energy of light can be expressed as $E = hv$, where h is the Plank's constant and v is the frequency.

45. D: Current can be expressed as the flow of charge per time, which Answers A and C both express. Answer B follows from the units in Ohm's law, $V = IR$. Answer D is the only incorrect way of expressing current, although watts per volts would be an OK way to express amperes, which follows from the Power equation $P = IV$.

46. B: For resistors in series, the total resistance is the sum of their individual resistances. For resistors in parallel, the total resistance is given by $1/R = 1/R_1 + 1/R_2 + \ldots$ First, the bottom two resistors have a total resistance of $2\ \Omega + 4\ \Omega = 6\ \Omega$. Then add this in parallel with

the 3 Ohm resistor. $1/R = 1/3 + 1/6 = 1/2$. So $R = 2\ \Omega$ for the bottom three elements. To find the total resistance, add this in series to the top resistor, for a total $R = 10\ \Omega + 2\Omega = 12\Omega$.

47. B: Answers A and C are wrong because they doesn't have the units of energy (joules). To make things easier, the correct answer follows the same form as other kinds of energy (KE = $\frac{1}{2}mv^2$, a spring's potential energy is $\frac{1}{2}kx^2$, etc.) The capacitance is defined as Q/V, so the energy is proportional to QV. The potential at a point in space is determined by the concentration of charge at that point, but the potential difference (V = work/charge) is defined in terms of the motion of a small test charge. At the very beginning of the process of charging up a capacitor, the work needed to move a test charge from the positive plate to the negative plate is 0 volts. As the capacitor charges up, more energy is required to move the charge because the charge is repelled by the negative plate. The total energy stored is Q × average voltage. Since the voltage increases linearly, the average voltage is $\frac{1}{2}\ V$.

48. A: The current that flows in the resistor connected to the battery without the capacitor is 5×10^{-5} ampere. When the battery is disconnected this is the initial current as the electrons flow from the negative plate through the resistor to the positive plate. As electrons build up on the positive plate, the current decreases. The decrease is exponential, so the capacitor never fully loses its charge. Answer B is the time constant for the RC circuit (resistance × capacitance). After 30 seconds, the current is 37% of its initial value. When the time lapsed is three times RC, the current will be reduced to 95%. Within a short time, the current will be so small it will not be measureable with an ammeter, although it will technically never fully discharge.

49. D: For constructive interference, the waves must arrive having the same phase. Therefore, neither Answers A or B can be correct. Constructive interference occurs when the waveforms add together, producing a maximum that is twice as intense as either of the individual waves. Answer C would cause the waves to be out of phase by 1, 3, 5 or 7 (etc.) half-wavelengths, meaning the waves would be out of phase by a half-wavelength. Only Answer D assures that the two waves arrive in phase.

50. C: A ray of sunlight consists of many different colors of light. The speed of red light in water is slightly larger than the speed of violet light, so the angle of refraction of violet light is greater than that of red light. This causes the light to separate and creates a spectrum of colors, like in a prism. Raindrops do exhibit total internal reflection for all the wavelengths inside the droplet, although this is not what causes the rainbow. Instead, this causes a second refraction as the sunlight emerges from the water droplet, which can sometimes been seen in nature as a "double rainbow."

51. D: Since the lens is convex, the focal length is positive and the image will appear behind the lens. You can use the lens equation to solve this. $1/f = 1/o + 1/i$, where f is the coal length, i is the image location and o is the object location. Since the object is in front it has a positive sign. $1/10$ cm = $1/20$ cm + $1/i$, so $1/i = 1/20$ and i = 20 cm. The positive sign for the image means that it is behind the lens.

52. B: This question is asking about a concave MIRROR, not a lens. Since light does not pass through a mirror—it only reflects off of it—the different colors of light all bend the same amount. If light was passing through a lens, the different colors would bend slightly different amounts, causing chromatic aberration. That's not the case here. Spherical

aberration occurs because the focal point of the mirror changes slightly as you move away from the center (optical axis). Astigmatism occurs when incident rays are not parallel to the optical axis. A circular beam, striking a lens or mirror at an angle to the optical axis, will become a parabola. Distortion concerns magnification and occurs in both mirrors and lenses.

Verbal Reasoning

1. B: France is a country on the continent of Europe and China is a country on the continent of Asia.

2. D: A fable is a type of story and a sandal is a type of shoe.

3. C: A shell can be found on the beach and a rock can be found on a mountain.

4. B: You cook in a kitchen and you read in a library.

5. D: A rug covers the floor and a sheet covers a bed

6. A: A smokestack extends from the roof of a factory and a steeple extends from the roof of a church.

7. C: Rain feels wet and fire feels hot.

8. D: Sentences make up a paragraph and bricks make up a wall.

9. A: Try is another word for attempt and challenge is another word for dare.

10. C: To laugh is to show joy and to sneer is to show contempt.

11. A: A surgeon works in a hospital and a clerk works in a store.

12. B: A basket can be made by weaving and a scarf can be made by knitting.

13. D: To eat is a solution to being hungry and to sleep is a solution to being tired.

14. D: A dune is a feature of the desert and a wave is a feature of the ocean.

15. A: Oil is applied to relieve a squeak and salve is applied to relieve a burn.

16. B: A nudge is less extreme as compared to a shove and nibble is less extreme as compared to devour.

17. C: A cavity is a flaw in a tooth and a wart is a flaw on the skin.

18. C: Had is the past tense of have and saw is the past tense of see.

19. D: A racket is used to play tennis and a paddle is used to play ping pong.

20. A: To etch is to embellish glass and to paint is to embellish a canvas.

21. C: "Short on money" is a clue that Glenda could not afford new appliances. Forgo means to do without. It makes sense that Glenda would forgo, or refrain from buying them.

22. B: The only two word choices which make any sense at all are subside and intensify. The next day's light breezes indicate that the winds would decrease, or subside, making subside the best choice. While it is possible that the already high winds could intensify, it is far more likely that the "light breezes" indicate that they did the opposite.

23. C: The sentence clearly states that Gloria was not hungry. All the answer choices except Choice C are indicative of hunger or excessive eating. It is far more likely that Gloria would have looked at her place *indifferently*.

24. A: Seminar and conference are the only two choices that make sense in the first blank so the other two choice can be eliminated. However, maritime is the only word that fits in the second answer blank, so Choice A is the correct answer.

25. E: Answer (a) is incorrect because it is not logically correct to speak of a problem's "positions." Answer (b) is incorrect because "all of its extreme" is not grammatically correct. Answer (c) is incorrect because it is not logically correct to speak of a problem's "thoughts." Answer (d) is grammatically correct, but because it is less common to "embrace" a problem than to "address" a problem, answer (e) is the better answer.

26. B: Answers (a), (d) and (e) are incorrect because the conjunction "but" in the sentence suggests that the second half happened despite the first half; in this answer, it doesn't logically make sense to say that numerous storylines were developed despite the thought-provoking nature of the book, that numerous plots were developed despite the surprising nature of the book, or that numerous chapters were developed despite the long-winded nature of the book. Answer (c) is incorrect because the second word, "answers," does not make sense in the context of the sentence. Answer (b) correctly links the two halves of the sentence: despite the brevity of the book, the author was able to develop numerous characters.

27. D: Answer (a) is incorrect because one would not repudiate true rumors. Answer (b) is incorrect; the phrase "to correction them" is not grammatically correct. Answer (c) is grammatically correct but does not make as much logical sense as answer (d). Answer (e) is incorrect; one does not demystify rumors.

28. A: Answers (b) and (e) are incorrect because one does not "look" arbitrary or abstruse. Answers (c) and (d) are grammatically correct, but answer (a) is the better answer because it explains why the speaker was sorry to see the object of the sentence: because she was despondent.

29. C: Answers (a) and (e) are incorrect because they suggest the disarray was minor; the opposite of the meaning suggested by the rest of the sentence. Answers (b) and (d) are incorrect because they offer information about the disarray that is not relevant to the rest of the sentence.

30. B: Answers (a) and (c) are incorrect because placid and obedient children are easy to care for, and would not logically be expected to frighten or enrage caretakers. Similarly, answers (d) and (e) are incorrect because truculent and egotistical children might be difficult to care for and would not logically be expected to appease or endear themselves to caretakers. Answer (e) is furthermore grammatically incorrect.

31. E: All the adjectives describing the house and the things in the house suggest a showy and grandiose home; ostentatious is the only answer choice that fits this meaning.

32. B: The word sought is one that describes something lucky that does not happen through design. Answer (b), serendipity, fits this meaning. Answer (a) is incorrect as it means the opposite of the word sought. Answers (c), (d) and (e) do not relate to the rest of the sentence.

33. E: Answers (a) and (d) are incorrect because their second words suggest he didn't *deny* a promotion when offered him, while the word that best fits the meaning of the sentence will be one that indicates that he didn't *seek* a promotion. Answers (c) and (e) offer words that fit this meaning, but answer (e) is better because ambition fits more logically into the sentence than does habits. Answer (b) is wrong because it is not logically correct to say he was modest in his failures.

34. A: Answers (b), (c) and (d) are incorrect as they all provide words that do not make logical sense describing an economic major ("literary," "theatrical," and "sycophantic"). Answer (e) is incorrect as it does not make logical sense that one avoiding a major because it felt unimportant would seek a more trivial one.

35. B: The correct answer is (b) prescient, which means able to anticipate the course of events. Answer (a) means early in development and is incorrect. Answer (c) means preceding in time and is incorrect. Answer (d) means related to a preface or located in front and is incorrect. Answer (e) means showing preference and is incorrect.

36. C: Answer (a) is incorrect because there is no context in the sentence for someone to discuss invisible footprints; additionally if the footprints were, despite invisibility, known of then it would be possible that the yeti had made them and the question wouldn't make sense. Answers (b), (d) and (e) are incorrect because there is no conflict between the words dangerous and massive, nor welcoming and cavernous, nor mysterious and unfathomable, and the sentence requires such conflict to make sense. Answer (c) is correct because the sentence appropriately poses the conflict of what could make such colossal footprints if the yeti does not exist.

37. D: The words sought are something a crowd does that then allows for an individual to walk in a certain way. Answers (a) and (b) are incorrect because a crowd thickening or intensifying does not lead to an individual being able to walk more confidently or on foot. Answer (c) is wrong because if the crowd has vanished, an individual is unable to walk en masse. Answer (e) is incorrect because neither word logically fits the sentence: a crowd does not startle and there is no context in the sentence to speak of the individual walking convincingly.

38. E: The part of the sentence provided indicates that the trip was such as to make the takers of it vow not to take another for some part of the future. Thus the first word should indicate that the trip was not a pleasant one; for this reason, answers (a), (d) and (e) are incorrect. Answer (b) is incorrect because the second word, so-called, does not logically complete the sentence.

39. B: The word "because" at the beginning of the sentence indicates that a reason is being given for the condition described in the second clause. Answer B logically completes the sentence: increasing demand for a limited resource leads to an increase in its value.

40. C: The second part of the sentence suggests that growth spurts and rapid physical changes disturb sleep patterns, so they are not likely to be "natural." Of the remaining choices, only "erratic" makes sense, and it provides a good description of a disturbed pattern.

Biological Sciences

1. B: Glycogen is a polysaccharide, a molecule composed of many bonded glucose molecules. Glucose is a carbohydrate, and all carbohydrates are composed of only carbon, oxygen, and hydrogen. Most other metabolic compounds contain other atoms, particularly nitrogen, phosphorous, and sulfur.

2. E: Endocytosis is a process by which cells absorb larger molecules or even tiny organisms, such as bacteria, than would be able to pass through the plasma membrane. Endocytic vesicles containing molecules from the extracellular environment often undergo further processing once they enter the cell.

3. A: Because the energy of the products is less than the energy of the substrate, the reaction releases energy and is an exergonic reaction.

4. B: The diploid chromosome number for humans is 46. After DNA duplication but before the first cell division of meiosis, there are 92 chromosomes (46 pairs). After meiosis I is completed, the chromosome number is halved and equals 46. Each daughter cell is haploid, but the chromosomes are still paired (sister chromatids). During meiosis II, the two sister chromatids of each chromosome separate, resulting in 23 haploid chromosomes per germ cell.

5. C: Genes code for proteins, and genes are discrete lengths of DNA on chromosomes. An allele is a variant of a gene (different DNA sequence.. In diploid organisms, there may be two versions of each gene.

6. C: Angiosperms produce flowers, with ovules inside of ovaries. The ovaries become a fruit, with seeds inside. Gymnosperms have naked seeds that are produced in cones or cone like structures.

7. C: Alternation of generations means the alternation between the diploid and haploid phases in plants.

8. C: Plants exchange gases with the environment through pores in their leaves called stomata. Animals exchange gases with the environment in many different ways: small animals like flatworms exchange gases through their skin; insects use tracheae; and many species use lungs.

9. B: Platelets are cell fragments that are involved in blood clotting. Platelets are the site for the blood coagulation cascade. Its final steps are the formation of fibrinogen which, when cleaved, forms fibrin, the "skeleton" of the blood clot.

10. A: HCG is secreted by the trophoblast, part of the early embryo, following implantation in the uterus. GnRH (gonadotropin-releasing hormone. is secreted by the hypothalamus, while LH (luteinizing hormone. and FSH (follicle-stimulating hormone. are secreted by the pituitary gland. GnRH stimulates the production of LH and FSH. LH stimulates ovulation and the production of estrogen and progesterone by the ovary in females, and testosterone

production in males. FSH stimulates maturation of the ovarian follicle and estrogen production in females and sperm production in males.

11. B: The gastrula is the first three-layered stage of the embryo, containing ectoderm, mesoderm, and endoderm

12. B: Carbon is released in the form of CO_2 through respiration, burning, and decomposition.

13. A: Pioneer species colonize vacant habitats, and the first such species in a habitat demonstrate primary succession. Succession on rock or lava often begins with lichens. Lichens need very little organic material and can erode rock into soil to provide a growth substrate for other organisms.

14. B: Character displacement means that, although similar, species in the same habitat have evolved characteristics that reduce competition between them. It occurs as a result of resource partitioning.

15. B: Adaptive radiation is the evolution of several species from a single ancestor. It occurs when a species colonizes a new area and members diverge geographically as they adapt to somewhat different conditions.

16. A: The first living organisms probably had not yet evolved the ability to synthesize their own organic molecules for food. They were probably heterotrophs that consumed nutrition from the "organic soup."

17. A: Proteins have a greater diversity of functions than any other biological molecules. It is nucleic acids that encode genetic information: proteins merely carry out the instructions encoded in genes.

18. B: The active site of an enzyme is a uniquely shaped three-dimensional space that is the site of biochemical reactions. Substrates fit within the active site in such a configuration that the enzyme and substrate can bind together. This union is called the enzyme-substrate complex. This pairing is very short lived because as soon as the chemical reaction that the enzyme catalyzes takes place, the enzyme and product dissociate.

19. C: In competitive inhibition, the competitor binds to the same active site as the substrate, preventing the substrate from binding. In feedback inhibition, an end product acts as an inhibitor: the question does not tell you that this has occurred. An allosteric enzyme has two binding sites, one for substrate (the active site) and one for effector (the allosteric site), and an allosteric inhibitor binds to the latter, not the former.

20. B: The three-dimensional structure of an enzyme is critical for its ability to bind substrates and catalyze reactions effectively. The three-dimensional structure is held in place by hydrogen bonds between amino acids, and these hydrogen bonds are easily disrupted, denaturing the protein (enzyme), by changes in temperature and pH.

21. A: During chemosmosis, energy from light is used to extract electrons from water and pump protons across the thylakoid membrane, creating a creating a proton gradient that

powers the generation of ATP and NADPH. Once these molecules are created, they power the processes described in alternatives B-E.

22. E: Short-day plants flower when day length is decreasing or night length is increasing. When plants are exposed to light during the night period, it resets their circadian-rhythm clocks and interferes with their calculation of night length.

23. A: The mouth produces salivary amylase, the enzyme that begins the breakdown of starch into maltose.

24. E: Muscle contraction (shivering) creates heat, so this would not be an effective way of maintaining body temperature in a hot environment.

25. D: A locus is defined as the location of a gene on a chromosome. Alleles of a gene are different forms of the same gene, and they have the same locus. Some alleles may be recessive and some may be dominant.

26. C: If two different traits are always inherited together, they do not segregate in meiosis and are linked.

27. C: A K-selected species has a population size that is constantly at or near carrying capacity. Its members produce few offspring, and the offspring are large and require extensive parental care until they mature.

28. E: Pollution affects the health of ecosystems and can limit population growth, but as it is a byproduct of human activity, it is not dependent on the density of the population.

29. B: Random mating would lead to an equilibrium of allele frequencies, while nonrandom mating (for example, inbreeding or sexual selection) would cause changes in allele frequencies.

30. E: Adaptive radiation is the evolution of several species from a single ancestor. It occurs when a species colonizes a new area and diverges as its members specialize for a particular set of conditions.

31. B: The endosymbiont theory, that early prokaryotes invaded other cells and took up residence there, is based on structure and function of current organelles. The fossil record does not provide direct evidence of this because early microscopic organisms would be unlikely candidates for fossilization.

32. A: The number of carbon and hydrogen atoms corresponds to the general formula for alkanes, C_nH_{2n+2}. This indicates that the compound is saturated and there are no double bonds to any carbon atoms. There can therefore only be single bonds involving the C and O atoms, which is satisfied only if the compound is an alcohol (one of thirteen possible isomers) or an ether (thirteen other possible isomers). Aldehydes and ketones have a double bond between a carbon atom and an oxygen atom and therefore cannot have a formula that agrees with the formula $C_6H_{14}O$.

33. D: The formula contains six carbon atoms and six hydrogen atoms. Structure a) corresponds to the formula C_6H_{12}. Structures b) and c) correspond to C_6H_8. Only structure d) of these possibilities corresponds to the formula C_6H_6.

34. B: In this reaction, the electron-rich C=C bond of 1-methylcyclohexene accepts a proton from the strong acid solution forming a C-H bond between one of the C=C carbon atoms and the H^+ ion. This results in the formation of a 2° carbonium ion at C2 if the C-H bond forms on C1 or a 3° carbonium ion at C1 if the C-H bond forms on C2. The process is a reversible equilibrium, and since a 3° carbonium ion is more stable than a 2° carbonium ion, any 2° ions formed would rearrange to the 3° ion structure. Addition of H_2O to the 3° carbonium ion, followed by loss of H^+, produces the product 1-methylcyclohexanol.

35. A: This is the definition of the carbonyl functional group. The term "carbonyl" refers specifically to the C=O group. The other three each contain a carbonyl group, but are not of themselves a carbonyl group. The carbonate group is the CO_3^{2-} ion, and the term "carbonate" is used to refer to salts and esters of the corresponding carbonic acid. The carboxylic function is the –COOH group. The acyl group is the carboxylic function without the -OH and can be represented by RCO. It is a carbonyl bonded to a carbon group (R). Ketones, aldehydes, esters and amides all contain acyl groups.

36. A: Optical isomers are properly termed enantiomers; molecules whose structures are exact mirror images of each other but that cannot be superimposed on each other. Such molecules have no planes or axes of symmetry, and are therefore asymmetric. An optically active compound may have only one isomer or it may have many. The number of possible isomers depends on the number of asymmetric carbon atoms in the molecule.

37. C: Enantiomeric isomers, or enantiomers, are molecules that are identical in every respect but are non-superimposable mirror images of each other according to the orientation of substituents about a central atom.
Geometric isomers are compounds that differ in their geometric structure only, for example, *cis-* and *trans-*2-butene.
Conformational isomers are the different shapes that can be adopted by a molecule, for example, the *chair*, *twist* and *boat* conformations of the cyclohexane molecule.
Structural isomers are compounds with the same molecular formula but different molecular structures, for example, C_2H_6O, which represents either ethanol, CH_3CH_2OH, or dimethyl ether, CH_3OCH_3.

38. A: Multiple bonds between two atoms bind the two together more tightly, bringing them closer together physically. Thus, they have shorter bond lengths. The total bond energy of a multiple bond is at minimum the sum of the energies of the individual bonds that make up the multiple bond. Therefore, they have higher bond energies according to their multiplicity. For example, the bond lengths and energies of bonds between carbon atoms follow the order:
C-C < C=C < C≡C
longest   shortest
Multiple bonds are sites of increased reactivity in molecules, especially as they are the defining feature of many different functional groups.
Bond lengths and energies are not relevant to molecular weights.

39. C: Chromatography of a tangible quantity of some mixture of compounds is used to separate those compounds from each other so that they can be collected in pure form. Small-scale chromatography is often used in laboratory procedures to monitor the progress of a reaction, usually through the disappearance of a compound as the reaction or other process progresses over time.

40. A: Caffeine is an alkaloid compound and therefore contains nitrogen. The –ine ending of the name indicates the presence of a nitrogen atom in the compound. The molecular structure shown contains no nitrogen and therefore cannot possibly be that of caffeine. The IUPAC name of the compound is 2-cyclohexyl-5-methylhept-4-en-3-one. It is, however, a conjugated enone, because the C=C bond and the C=O bond are separated from each other by a single C-C bond.

41. A: The C=O bond stretching absorption appears in IR spectra in the range of 1760 – 1670 cm^{-1}.
The CN bond absorption of nitriles appears in the range 2260 – 2220 cm^{-1}
The C-O-C bond absorption of ethers appears in the range 1260 – 1000 cm^{-1}.
The C=C bond absorption of alkenes appears in the range 1680 – 1640 cm^{-1}.

42. B: The mechanism of a reaction in which a nucleophile displaces another from an sp^3 carbon atom with inversion of the stereochemistry of the other three substituents is called a bimolecular nucleophilic substitution reaction. The mechanism is indicated by the S_N2 tag. An S_N1 reaction proceeds by loss of a nucleophile from a molecule, forming a carbonium ion intermediate.
The E1 and E2 reactions are elimination reactions and not substitution reactions.

43. C: In all forms of chromatography, the separation of components in a mixture is achieved by the differential rates at which the compounds adsorb and desorb from the surfaces of the stationary phase particles. The more times this can happen as the mixture progresses down the column, the better the separation of the components.
Solubility plays a role in chromatography but does not solely determine the separation of the components.
Similarly, polarity plays a role in chromatography but does not solely determine the separation of components.
Absorption is a different process than adsorption and is not involved in chromatography.

44. A: Sugar molecules are polyhydroxy aldehydes and ketones in their linear forms. They can form a cyclic structure by an intramolecular reaction that produces a cyclic hemiacetal or hemiketal structure. These cyclic structures are either five- or six-membered oxygen-heterocyclic rings. They are not bicyclic.
Sugar molecules can bond together very easily and are often found naturally in that form, like sucrose, starches and celluloses. Simple sugars that are naturally crystalline are easily recrystallized. Others tend to be thick, syrupy liquids rather than crystalline solids.

45. B: Grignard reagents are formed by the reaction of alkyl and aryl halides with magnesium metal in an anhydrous oxygenated solvent such as diethyl ether or tetrahydrofuran. A radical mechanism splits the carbon-halogen bond in such a way that the alkyl or aryl radical and the halogen radicals coordinate to a magnesium atom to form alkyl (or aryl) magnesium halide.

A Grignard reaction occurs when an appropriate Grignard reagent is reacted with a substrate molecule, such as a carbonyl compound. Grignard reactions are used to add structures to other molecules.
Magnesium bromide ($MgBr_2$) is one of the disposable by-products of Grignard reactions.

46. A:

1 – (2-methylpropyl)

Cyclohexyl 2-methylpropyl ether

1 – Bromocyclohexanol

47. D: All three are different names for the same compound produced by this reaction.

48. A: The lone pair electrons on the N atom of an amide are stabilized by delocalization into the carbonyl group ⯑ system. The orbital hybridization of the N atom is thus stabilized as $sp^2 + p$, which has trigonal planar geometry. Rotation about the amide C-N bond is restricted by the p orbital overlap.

49. B: Phosphines do not add to imines and phosphine oxides do not add to the carbonyl group.
The Wittig reaction involves the attack of the carbonyl group of a ketone or aldehyde by a phosphinium ylide, which results in the production of an alkene and a phosphine oxide byproduct. Typically, a triphenyl phosphinium ylide is used as a Wittig reagent. The carbon group of the Wittig reagent forms the double bond of the alkene in the same location as the carbonyl of the reactant ketone or aldehyde.

50. B: The Williamson synthesis produces ethers by the reaction of sodium alkoxides and alkyl halides. The reaction proceeds via an S_N2 mechanism. The alkoxide is produced by treatment of an alcohol with a very strong base such as sodium hydride to extract the –OH proton. An alkyl halide is then added to the solution, and the alkoxide ion nucleophile displaces the halide to form the ether product.

51. A: All steroids have the 6-6-6-5 ring structure in answer a). The other three structures are not steroidal, although they do have some similarities.